KENTUCKY
Dining by the Lakes

by

Paula Cunningham and Meredith Eddy

McClanahan
Publishing House

Cover design and book layout by James Asher Graphics
Project Manager, Michelle Stone
Editor, Alfred Imhoff

Manufactured in the United States of America

All book order correspondence should be addressed to:

McClanahan Publishing House, Inc.
P. O. Box 100
Kuttawa, KY 42055
(502) 388-9388
1-800-544-6959

to
Bill and Hank

Introduction

With the creation of Lake Barkley, Kentucky Lake, and the Land Between the Lakes, West Kentucky has become known as a recreational paradise. Families and retirees are moving into the region in droves, and more and more vacationers and sportsmen are targeting the area as a perfect place to camp, hunt, fish, boat, water ski, and sightsee.

The new residents and travelers have brought their appetites with them, and a plethora of restaurants has sprung up to satisfy the need. While traditional Southern cooking is still the strong favorite in the area, more and more ethnic eateries and upscale gourmet restaurants are being established. Down home barbecue diners abound, and seafood lovers are sure to enjoy the several places that specialize in fresh seafood.

In West Kentucky the only question is where do we eat? With such a wide assortment of possibilities, the choice becomes difficult. Hence *Kentucky: Dining by the Lakes*, which provides detailed information about stand-out West Kentucky restaurants plus some of the cherished recipes of the house.

In many instances, restaurants have given us some of their best and most requested favorites. In others, owners have shared family treasures that have been enjoyed by generations. In either case, *Kentucky: Dining by the Lakes* supplies the home cook with enough ammunition to serve up favorites from the region for many years to come.

We hope you enjoy the dining out suggestions and recipes as much as we enjoyed doing the research, and sampling our way through some of the best restaurants in West Kentucky.

Paula Cunningham
Meredith Eddy

Contents

In 1796, a North Carolinian named Bartholomew Wood erected a log cabin in the Pennyrile region of West Kentucky. Wood later donated five acres of land to the growing community of Christian county to be used for public buildings. Bartholomew's Restaurant sits on the site of his original log cabin.

The grand old building that now houses the restaurant is built of brick, stone, and terra cotta and was completed in 1894. Known then as the Racket Store, it was a town center where buggies and general merchandise were sold. The building was placed on the National Register in 1979.

The nostalgic atmosphere of Bartholomew's sets the mood for fine dining in a comfortable setting. The interior is filled with greenery, antiques, old gas street lamps, and historical town pictures hanging from the old walls. There is even a picture of Bartholomew T. Wood, son of the founder, and a copy of the original deed to the property. The pride the owners take in the restaurant is evident in the high-quality food and courteous service that are the hallmarks of Bartholomew's.

The menu offers excellent charbroiled burgers topped with Bartholomew's special honey-mustard dressing, sandwiches, and a wide assortment of salads — from Chicken Pineapple to Grilled Chicken Salad. The Loaded Potato Soup, a house specialty, is served with a freshly baked croissant drizzled with honey butter. Entrees such as Chicken Santa Fe, Mandarin

Bartholomew's

Pork Chops, and Beef Kabobs are made with the finest in fresh ingredients and served in generous portions. Tortellini Marinara, Chicken Enchiladas, and Shrimp Alfredo are served with house-made sauces, and will leave barely enough room for the famous Toll House Pie and a hot cappuccino or espresso coffee.

The bar upstairs is a gathering place for friends after working hours, and is known for its specialty drinks like Strawberry Shortcake and Bartholomew's Country Smash. Bartholomew's pleases guests and continues to be a special place for people who want to share good times and good food in a unique atmosphere.

Bartholomew's has proved so successful over the years

that a second restaurant has been opened in Madisonville. In operation for over two years, it features the same delicious menu and fine dining atmosphere as the flagship restaurant in Hopkinsville.

Banquet rooms are available at both locations, and the management promises that the food and service will make the largest company luncheon meeting or the most intimate rehearsal dinner an occasion to enjoy and remember.

Proprietor: South Main Restaurant Corp.

Addresses: 914 S. Main Street, Hopkinsville, KY 42240. 51 S. Main Street, Madisonville, KY 42431.

Telephone: Hopkinsville: (502) 886-5768. Madisonville: (502) 821-1061.

Hours: Lunch, Monday through Friday, is 11:00 a.m. to 2:30 p.m. Dinner, Monday through Thursday, is 5:00 p.m. to 9:30 p.m.; Friday until 11:00 p.m. Saturday hours are 11:00 a.m. to 11:00 p.m.

Season: Open year round.

Seating: Reservations not accepted; call ahead for preferred seating. The banquet room in Hopkinsville is located on the second floor and seats up to 50 people. In Madisonville, the banquet room is located on the second-floor mezzanine and can accommodate up to 70 people.

Credit cards: Visa, MasterCard, American Express, and Discover.

Directions: Hopkinsville: located downtown on the corner of 10th and S. Main streets. Madisonville: located downtown on the corner of S. Main and Sugg streets.

Chicken Tortilla Soup

3 red onions, chopped fine
1/8 cup minced garlic
1/8 cup vegetable oil
3/4 gallon of water
1/3 cup chicken base (or instant bullion)
3/4 chopped red bell pepper
3 teaspoons chili powder
2 1/2 teaspoons basil
1 1/2 teaspoons black pepper
2 quarts stewed, chopped tomatoes
8 skinned and boned chicken breasts
tortilla chips
Monterey Jack cheese

Sauté onions and garlic in vegetable oil, stirring occasionally, until onions are tender. Boil chicken, reserving 3/4 gallon of broth. Chop chicken into bite-sized pieces. Combine broth, water, chicken bouillon, bell pepper, chili powder, basil, pepper, and tomatoes. Bring to a boil, then reduce heat and simmer uncovered for 30 minutes. Add chicken, and ladle into individual serving bowls. Add tortilla chips to each bowl and top with grated Monterey Jack cheese.

Serves 12

Spinach and Artichoke Dip

1 4-ounce jar artichoke hearts
5 ounces chopped frozen spinach, thawed
1 can cream of mushroom soup
1/4 cup grated Parmesan cheese
1/2 cup mayonnaise
1 pinch garlic powder
1 pinch onion salt
1 pinch salt
1 pinch white pepper
1 cup grated Monterey Jack cheese

Drain and chop artichoke hearts. Drain water from spinach. Mix all ingredients. Place in baking dish and bake at 350 degrees for 15 minutes until lightly browned.

Serves 20

To give this appetizer a little something extra, try topping it with sour cream and chopped chives. A party pleaser!

Marinated Beef Kabobs

2 cups soy sauce
1 46-ounce can pineapple juice
1/2 tablespoon ground ginger
1 5-ounce bottle Worcestershire sauce
1 tablespoon granulated garlic
1 cup sugar
2 pounds beef kabobs
green peppers, cored and cut into quarters
cherry tomatoes
red onions, cut into quarters
whole mushrooms

Place all ingredients except kabobs and vegetables in glass container and mix with wire whip. Place the meat in the marinade and leave for at least eight hours. Thread marinated beef on skewers with vegetables and grill.

Makes 2 quarts marinade

Seafood Pasta Sauce

1/2 pound butter or margarine
1/8 cup minced garlic
1 cup flour
1 1/2 quarts heavy whipping cream
4 ounces lobster base (or seafood bouillon)
1 quart half-and-half cream
2 cups water
1/2 cup white wine

Melt butter and cook garlic on low heat for 2 to 3 minutes. Add flour and cook roux on low heat for 5 minutes. Add heavy cream, half and half, lobster base, and water, stirring constantly. Simmer until sauce thickens, stirring occasionally. Add wine and remove from heat.

Serves 6

Add shrimp, crab, scallops, or lobster to taste and serve over pasta!

Carole's Award–Winning Old–Fashioned Lemonade

1 teaspoon sugar
1/4 lemon, seeded but unpeeled
Splash of 7-Up
Splash of sweet and sour mix
1 ounce vodka (optional)

Place all ingredients in a blender and mix until the lemon is grated. Pour over ice.

Serves 1

The Bluegrass Steak House & Seafood is a hungry person's paradise. Specializing in steak and seafood dinners, the restaurant also welcomes the lunch crowd with plate dinners served from 11:00 a.m. to 2:00 p.m. A special plate is also offered daily, featuring an entrée such as fried chicken or pork chops, three choices of vegetables, coleslaw, and corn bread for a very reasonable price. Sandwiches, served all day, range from the Bluegrass Burger to more exotic offerings like Chicken Divan on pita bread.

The Bluegrass Steak House & Seafood is owned and operated by George and Jenny Xakis, both originally from Greece, and the influence of their home country can be found on the menu. Gyros are available in a sandwich or a plate dinner, and Greek salad and beef kabobs are also on the menu.

The steaks are big and juicy and cooked to order. Try the large T-bone, large ribeye, New York strip, or ground sirloin. Catfish is served in a variety of delicious presentations, including fillets, fiddlers, baked lemon pepper fish, Cajun-style, and Parmesan fillets. A number of chicken dishes and specialty steak (steak & shrimp, smoked chops) dinners are on the menu as well, all served with a choice of potato and salad.

There is a wide variety of seafood dinners. Try the baked orange roughy, grilled salmon steaks, stuffed shrimp, fried oysters, fried clams, or stuffed flounder. For a lighter dinner, try one of the many salads on the menu, such as Greek, chef's, or crabmeat. Children love having their own menu, and can choose chicken strips, a hamburger, or chicken a patty. Dessert offerings include pecan, apple, and meringue pie, or a slice of delicious cheesecake.

Bluegrass Steak House & Seafood

The comfortable atmosphere at the Bluegrass Steak House & Seafood provides a relaxing place to stop for everybody from truckers on the road to tired shoppers from the West Kentucky Factory Outlet Mall across the street. The three dining areas are roomy and open, and display signed publicity photos of country-western stars who have passed through town.

The ever-full parking lot outside the Bluegrass Steak

House attests to its continued draw and hearty good food. The congenial hosts and friendly waitresses make the dining experience that much more pleasant. And the grilled steaks and seafood keep people coming back for more!

Proprietors: George and Jenny Xakis.

Address: U.S. Highways 62 & 93, Eddyville, KY 42038.

Telephone: (502) 388-2468.

Hours: Open from 11:00 a.m. to 10:00 p.m. in summer; 11:00 a.m. to 9:00 p.m. in winter.

Season: Open year round; closed Thanksgiving and Christmas Days.

Seating: No reservations necessary.

Credit cards: Not accepted.

Directions: Located across from the West Kentucky Factory Outlet Mall at the intersection of U. S. Highways 62 & 93 in Eddyville.

Pastitsio

1 pound ground beef
1 onion, diced
1 cup water
1 small can (8 ounces) tomato sauce
1 pound spaghetti
1/2 cup Parmesan cheese
1 stick butter
6 tablespoons flour
3 eggs
3 cups milk
1 teaspoon nutmeg
dash salt
dash pepper

Brown ground beef in skillet in one tablespoon butter, adding onion and cooking until onion is limp. Drain fat, then add water and tomato sauce. Let simmer for 45 minutes. In the meantime, cook spaghetti in boiling, salted water until tender and drain. Place cooked spaghetti in a 24-inch baking pan that has been greased with butter. Cover with beef mixture and sprinkle with 1/4 cup Parmesan cheese. Melt butter in saucepan. Add flour, stirring about 4 minutes until well blended. Beat eggs and add to milk. Slowly add egg mixture to flour mixture, stirring well, and simmer until sauce is thickened. Add nutmeg, salt, and pepper and blend well. Pour sauce over ground beef casserole, and sprinkle with remaining Parmesan cheese. Bake at 300 degrees for 45 minutes.

Serves 6 to 8

Leg of Lamb Marinade

1 leg of lamb, butterflied
1 cup honey
1 cup soy sauce
8 cloves garlic, crushed

Have the butcher butterfly a leg of lamb. Mix the honey, soy sauce, and garlic and marinate the lamb overnight, covered, in the refrigerator. Grill over hot coals until just done.

Serves 8

This is an extraordinarily easy summer entrée to prepare, yet wonderfully elegant for a dinner party! Fabulous when served with sliced cucumbers in yogurt sauce and a minty tabouleh salad.

Greek Salad

Salad:
1/2 head romaine lettuce, torn in pieces
1/2 head red leaf lettuce, torn in pieces
1 tomato, cut in wedges
1 cup thinly sliced red onion
1 cup thinly sliced cucumber
1/2 cup shredded carrots
1 cup crumbled feta cheese
1/2 cup Greek olives

Dressing:
1/2 cup olive oil
1/4 cup red wine vinegar
1 tablespoon prepared mustard
1/2 teaspoon oregano
1 clove garlic, minced

Combine salad ingredients. In a separate bowl, combine dressing ingredients and stir with a wire whip. Pour dressing over salad. Toss well.

Serves 4

Shrimp and Rice Pilaf

2 onions, diced
1/2 cup olive oil
1/4 teaspoon salt
1/2 teaspoon pepper
1/4 teaspoon oregano
1 small can (8 ounces) tomato sauce
1 1/2 cups rice
1 pound shrimp, peeled and deveined

Sauté onions in oil until limp. Add spices and tomato sauce, and simmer for ten to twenty minutes. Boil or steam rice in separate pot until done; drain. Add shrimp to tomato sauce mixture and cook until done. Put rice in serving bowl and top with shrimp and sauce.

Serves 6

Greek–Style Baked Chicken

1 chicken, cut up
6 red potatoes, quartered
oregano to taste
salt to taste
pepper to taste
garlic powder to taste
juice from 5 lemons
1/2 cup water
1/2 stick butter

Wash chicken and pat dry. Place in baking pan and sprinkle with spices. Surround chicken with potato wedges, and season again with spices to taste. Mix lemon juice and water and sprinkle over chicken and potatoes. Dot potatoes and chicken with butter. Bake at 350 degrees for 60 minutes.

Serves 4

For a truly authentic Kentucky experience, locals know to shop at Broadbent's Foods & Gifts store. Visitors to the Bluegrass State quickly discover that country hams are as traditional to Kentucky as Thoroughbred horses and fine bourbon whiskey. For over eighty-five years the Broadbent family has been growing hogs and curing country hams, bacon, and sausage on the Broadbent Farm.

Winners of the Kentucky State Fair Grand Champion Ham award seven times, Broadbent's country hams have also received the coveted Grand Champion Ham award at the Mid-South State Fair in Memphis, Tennessee.

Smith Broadbent, Sr., and then Smith, Jr., grew hogs on the Broadbent Farm and cured them for friends and family. Grandsons Smith III and Bob later adapted the old ways to more modern methods and expanded the business into the Broadbent's B&B Food Products company that is so successful today. They are one of the only commercial ham producers in Kentucky who do everything from raising their own hogs in climate-controlled buildings under sanitary conditions to curing the products by hand the old-fashioned way with extended aging and gentle smoking with hickory and sassafras.

Hams are available through the B&B catalog or at Broadbent's Foods & Gifts store. B&B's other down home country foods are also available there, including such delicacies as smoked slab bacon and smoked country pork sausage seasoned to taste-tempting perfection

Broadbent's Foods & Gifts

using Grandma Broadbent's secret eighty-five-year-old recipe.

The country store is a cornucopia of authentic Kentucky gift items, from Bourbon Pecan Cake to country mixes for biscuits, pancakes, corn bread, and spoon bread. Homemade jams, jellies, and preserves make wonderful souvenirs, and the ready-to-eat summer sausage and farm cheese are all that's needed for a spontaneous country picnic!

All in all, B&B produces more than five-hundred country and gourmet food products, all with the B&B guarantee of quality. The store also offers an excellent selection of gifts, custom food baskets, and accessories for all occasions.

The store is open seven days a week and is a must-see for visitors to West Kentucky. If you are unable to stop by, a full color catalog is free upon request by writing to the store. All products are shipped nationwide, and a discount is given on quantity orders. The catalog contains many ideas for unique gifts and provides a wide selection of foods to please the most discriminating palate.

Proprietor: Broadbent's B&B Food Products, Inc.

Address: 5695 Hopkinsville Rd., Cadiz, KY 42211.

Telephone: (502) 522-6674. Out-of-state orders 1-800-841-2202.

Hours: April through December: Sunday through Thursday 8:00 a.m. to 7:00 p.m., Friday and Saturday 8:00 a.m. to 8:00 p.m. January through March: Sunday through Thursday 8:00 a.m. to 5:30 p.m., Friday and Saturday 8:00 a.m. to 6:30 p.m.

Season: Open year round.

Credit cards: American Express, MasterCard, Visa, and Discover.

Directions: Five miles east of Cadiz on U.S. Highway 68 at the Interstate 24 junction (exit 65). Located in west Kentucky near Barkley Lake and Land Between the Lakes. Approximately 55 miles southeast of Paducah, and 70 miles northwest of Nashville.

Kentucky Hot Brown

1 tablespoon butter or margarine
2 tablespoons all-purpose flour
1 cup milk
1/8 teaspoon chicken-flavored bouillon granules
2 tablespoons shredded cheddar cheese
3 ounces thinly sliced cooked turkey breast
3 ounces thinly sliced cooked country ham
2 slices bread, toasted
2 slices bacon, cooked
1 slice tomato
1 teaspoon grated Parmesan cheese
paprika
fresh parsley

Melt butter in a heavy saucepan over low heat, add flour, and cook 1 minute, stirring constantly. Gradually adding milk and bouillon granules, cook over medium heat, stirring constantly until thickened. Add cheddar cheese, and stir until cheese melts. Set aside.

Warm turkey and ham in skillet. Place 1 piece of toast in the center of an overproof plate. Cut remaining piece of toast in half, and place one-half on each side of the plate. Cover toast with turkey and ham. Spoon cheese sauce over meat, and bake at 300 degrees for 10 minutes. Top with bacon and tomato, and bake an additional 5 minutes. Sprinkle with Parmesan cheese and paprika. Garnish with parsley.

Serves 2

Country Ham Loaves

1 1/2 cups ground cooked country ham
1/2 cup mayonnaise
6 slices day-old bread
1 1/2 cups (6 ounces) shredded sharp cheddar cheese
1/2 cup plus 2 tablespoons butter or margarine, softened

Combine ham and mayonnaise; mix well. Spread ham mixture over 4 slices of bread; stack 2 spread slices on top of each other. Top each sandwich with remaining slice of bread; cut each sandwich in half.

Combine cheese and butter and mix until well blended. Frost top and sides of each sandwich with cheese mixture and refrigerate several hours. Place a wire rack on a baking sheet; place ham loaves on rack. Bake at 450 degrees for 2 minutes or until cheese melts.

Serves 4

Kentucky Jack

2 (1/4-inch-thick) slices uncooked country ham
2 tablespoons water
4 slices tomato
2 English muffins, halved and toasted
4 (1-ounce) slices cheddar cheese
4 (1-ounce) slices Swiss cheese

Place ham in a large skillet over medium heat. Add water, and fry 4 to 5 minutes on each side. Remove ham slices from skillet; add tomatoes to skillet and grill lightly.

Place equal amounts of ham over each muffin half. Top each with a slice of tomato, cheddar cheese, and Swiss cheese. Place on a baking sheet and broil 1 to 2 minutes or until cheese melts.

Serves 4

Gourmet Chicken Breast with Country Ham

1 whole chicken breast, boned and cut in half
2 slices baked or boiled country ham, thinly sliced
1 can cream of mushroom soup
1 small can mushrooms
2 tablespoons dry white wine

Wrap each chicken breast half with a slice of country ham and secure with toothpicks. Place in a shallow greased baking dish. Pour the undiluted soup into a bowl and briskly stir the wine and mushrooms into it. Pour the mixture over the chicken breasts and bake in a preheated 250-degree oven for 2 to 2 1/2 hours.

Serves 2

Tucked in the west end of Broadbent's Foods & Gifts is a delightful cafe where a hungry shopper can enjoy a quick bite or a slow, relaxing meal. On sunny days the adjoining solarium with overhead fans quickly fills up as diners enjoy the freshly-prepared meals, all made from scratch that morning, in the bright sunshine.

The proprietor of Broadbent Cafe, John Franklin, started his career in food preparation at the age of thirteen. He ran a guest house in Kleinottweiler, Germany, an experience that widened his skills in preparing different foods. Daughter Jill also loves to cook and has created some of the items that appear on the menu.

The menu features all of the meats from Broadbent's B&B Food Products, including fried country ham, cold baked ham, country-cured bacon, and sausage, as well as vegetables and soups seasoned with the country meat products. The Grand Champion breakfast features country ham and fresh eggs, along with hash browns or grits and homemade biscuits. The Broadbent Platter offers a choice of smoked bacon, city ham, or smoked sausage, and is also accompanied by homemade biscuits or toast. Those with lighter appetites can try Jill's French Toast or yogurt with low-fat granola and seasonal fresh fruits.

Specials appear on the menu each day. Diners enjoy exciting creations such as Fruited Chicken Salad, Pasta Salad, Homemade Texas Hot Chili, and other

Broadbent Cafe

freshly created soups and salads. Sandwiches served on homemade bread are made with meats that are cooked and seasoned in house, making them a cut above the usual offering.

The dessert cart bulges with varied homemade treats. The pies and other specials change daily, and repeat patrons look for desserts such as the Praline Cheesecake and Chocolate/Strawberry Torte. Desserts are John Franklin's specialty and all who are fortunate to taste them acknowledge he is a master at creating them.

An old-fashioned fountain dispenses ice cream treats made with lots of nuts and whipped cream. Choose from fourteen ice cream flavors and six fresh toppings, and then decide between ice cream floats, sundaes, hot fudge cake or the indomitable banana split.

Though small in size, Broadbent Cafe is big on flavor and unique tastes. Stop by before or after shopping in Broadbent's for an unforgettable dining experience!

BROADBENT
CAFE

Proprietor: John Franklin.

Address: 5695 Hopkinsville Road, Cadiz, KY 42211.

Telephone: (502) 522-3156.

Hours: Sunday through Thursday 6:30 a.m. to 7:00 p.m., Friday and Saturday 6:30 a.m. to 8:00 p.m.

Season: Open year round. Closed Easter, Thanksgiving, Christmas Day and New Year's Day.

Seating: No reservations necessary.

Credit cards: Visa, MasterCard, American Express, and Discover.

Directions: Exit 65 off of Interstate 24 at the intersection of U.S. Highway 68 in the west end of Broadbent's Foods & Gifts country store.

Jill's French Toast

6 large eggs
1 cup half-and-half cream
1 tablespoon sugar
1 teaspoon cinnamon
1/8 teaspoon nutmeg
1 teaspoon vanilla
24 slices French bread, cut 3/4 inch thick

Blend first six ingredients well. Dip French bread in mixture, coating both sides. Cook in pan or on griddle sprayed with vegetable oil over medium heat until both sides are golden brown. Serve with butter and maple syrup or fruit preserves.

Serves 6

Chicken Enchiladas

2 cups sour cream
2 16-ounce cans tomatoes
1 10-ounce jar pepperoncini
1 teaspoon coriander seed
1 teaspoon salt
2 cups finely chopped cooked chicken breast, preferably marinated or smoked
1/2 cup freshly chopped onion
6 ounces softened cream cheese
1 1/2 teaspoons salt
4 tablespoons vegetable oil
24 6-inch soft flour tortillas
2 cups shredded sharp cheddar cheese
leaf lettuce
commercial salsa

To make sauce: Place first 5 ingredients in food processor and blend until mixture is well combined and fairly smooth. Set aside.

Combine chicken, cream cheese, onion, and 1 1/2 teaspoons salt in bowl. Divide chicken mixture between tortillas. Roll up each tortilla and place seam side down in baking dish. Pour sauce over top. Cover and bake at 350 degrees for 30 minutes.

Place two enchiladas on a plate garnished with leaf lettuce. Sprinkle each one with cheddar cheese and a tablespoon of salsa.

Serves 12

Lemon Meringue Pie

Pie filling:
1 cup sugar
1/2 cup cornstarch
1/2 cup lemon juice
granted rind of one lemon
1 1/2 cups warm water
4 egg yolks, slightly beaten
1 tablespoon butter

Meringue:
4 egg whites
1/4 teaspoon cream of tartar
8 tablespoons sugar
1 9-inch baked pie crust

In medium saucepan, combine first five ingredients. Using wire whisk stir and cook over medium heat until mixture begins to boil and thicken. Remove from heat. Pour a small amount of mixture into egg yolks, stirring well. Stir egg mixture back into saucepan and whisk in butter. Pour into baked pie shell.

To make meringue: Beat egg whites and cream of tartar on high, adding sugar 1 tablespoon at a time until stiff peaks form. Top lemon pie with meringue, making sure the filling is hot and edges are sealed. Bake at 400 degrees for 10 minutes.

Serves 8

Pie Crust

2 1/2 cups all-purpose flour
1/8 teaspoon salt
1 cup chilled shortening or butter
7 tablespoons cold water

Place flour, salt, and shortening or butter in food processor. Using pulse setting, blend until mixture resembles coarse meal. Add water, 1 tablespoon at a time, using short spurts. Dough will ball up and leave sides of processor upon reaching proper consistency. Turn out on floured surface and form into a ball. Divide in half. Makes enough for 2 one-crust pies or 1 two-crust pie.

For baked pie shell, preheat oven to 400 degrees and bake for 10 minutes or until crust begins to brown.

Makes 2 pie crusts

Broadbent Cafe is known for its elegant, homemade desserts. The chef receives numerous compliments on his light and flaky pie crusts!

Travelers from around the country will tell you that never have they encountered two friendlier people than Catfish Kitchen owners Wes and Judy Davis. Their congenial hospitality, the casual country atmosphere of the restaurant, and the delicious food easily account for the jam-packed parking lot and repeat customers!

Situated on a graceful, ten-acre lake divided by a levee, Catfish Kitchen is decorated with antiques and country memorabilia that change whenever Judy gets the whim. The non-smoking Nautical Room is decorated with waterside bric-a-brac and fishing nets, and has a lovely view of the lake. The main dining room also overlooks the lake and has big picture windows on all sides. The restaurant accommodates 110 diners at cozy picnic-style tables.

Just about everything on the menu at Catfish Kitchen — from the delicious breading on the fried catfish to the famous Catfish Kitchen Hot Sauce — is homemade, and patrons enjoy the fresh and tasty quality of the food. Fried chicken, catfish, shrimp, and frog leg dinners are the house specialties, served with coleslaw, hush puppies or biscuits, beans, and choice of potatoes. Low-fat baked fish and chicken dinners are served by call-ahead order, and special menus are available for senior citizens and children under 12.

The all-you-can eat combo fried catfish and chicken dinner is very popular with customers,

Catfish Kitchen

as are the munchies on the menu — pickled green tomatoes and country-fried dill pickles. Those who like a little heat with their dinners order Hornets, breaded, cheese-stuffed jalapeno peppers, or Hot Pups, jalapeno hush puppies guaranteed to wake up your taste buds.

A rustic, covered porch jutting out over the lake serves as the launching pad for the catfish feeders. Wes and Judy save day-old hush puppies and give them to children, who delight in watching the fat catfish (weighing up to 30 pounds) rise to the surface to grab them. Add the graceful flocks of Canadian Geese that fly over the lake and settle on the levee, and one finds a pastoral setting that is both relaxing and entertaining for the entire family.

Don't leave Catfish Kitchen without trying the fabulous, homemade desserts, like Grandma Minnie's pies and Aunt Ju-Ju's fruit cobblers. For a special treat, order them warm with ice cream à la mode!

Catfish Kitchen is open year round from Wednesday through Sunday. With advance registration, special parties can book the restaurant on Mondays and Tuesdays.

Proprietors: Wes and Judy Davis.

Address: 136 Teal Run Circle, Benton, KY 42025.

Telephone: (502) 362-7306.

Hours: Open Wednesday through Saturday from 4:00 p.m. to 9:00 p.m. Open Sundays from 11:00 a.m. to 9:00 p.m.

Season: Open year round.

Seating: Call ahead waiting is available. Diners can call the restaurant before leaving home and have their names placed on a waiting list.

Credit cards: MasterCard and Visa.

Directions: Five miles south of Kentucky Dam on U.S. Highway 641. Restaurant is located on the right.

Quick Taco Casserole

1 1/2 pounds ground beef
1/2 onion, chopped
1 package taco seasoning mix
1 can cream of mushroom soup
1 can Ro-Tel tomatoes
1 package tortilla chips
1 cup grated cheddar cheese

Brown meat and onion in skillet; drain. Add taco seasoning mix, mushroom soup, and Ro-Tel tomatoes. Place chips in casserole dish, add meat mixture, and top with grated cheese. Bake at 350 degrees until cheese melts.

Serves 6

Almond Chicken Pasta Salad

4 cups cooked, cubed chicken
2 cups cored and coarsely chopped apples
8 ounces corkscrew or bow-tie pasta, cooked and drained
1 - 8 1/2 ounce can pineapple chunks, drained
1/2 cup halved, seedless grapes
1/3 cup bias-sliced celery
1/4 cup mayonnaise
1/3 cup low-fat plain yogurt
1 tablespoon sesame seeds
1 teaspoon finely shredded lime peel
3 tablespoons lime juice
1 tablespoon honey
1/4 teaspoon salt
1/2 cup toasted, sliced almonds
lettuce leaves

In large bowl, toss together the cooked chicken, apples, cooked pasta, pineapple, grapes, and celery. In a separate bowl, mix mayonnaise, yogurt, sesame seeds, lime peel, lime juice, honey and salt. Pour over pasta mixture and toss gently to combine. Cover and chill. To serve, add several tablespoons of milk to moisten if necessary. Toss gently. Serve on lettuce-lined plates. Top with almonds. If desired, garnish with lime slices, avocado, and sliced sweet pepper.

Serves 10

Social Chicken Casserole

1 cup sliced mushrooms
1 tablespoon butter
1 can cream of mushroom soup
8 ounces sour cream
1 package dried French onion dip mix
1 stewed chicken, with meat pulled from bone and cut in bite-sized pieces
1/2 package Pepperidge Farm stuffing mix

Sauté mushrooms briefly in butter and set aside. Mix together cream of mushroom soup, sour cream and dip mix. Add chicken and mushrooms, mix well and place in casserole dish. Cover with stuffing mix. Bake at 350 degrees for 25 minutes in covered casserole dish, then remove cover and bake another 10 minutes.

Serves 6

This dish is easy to prepare and draws rave reviews at socials and potluck suppers. Stew six skinless, boneless chicken breasts instead of a whole chicken to cut down on preparation time.

Cherry Cream Freeze

1 can cherry pie filling
3/4 cup crushed, drained pineapple
1 can sweetened, condensed milk
1/4 teaspoon vanilla
1/4 cup lemon juice
2 cups whipped topping

Mix all ingredients except whipped topping in a large bowl. Fold in the topping and place the mixture in a dessert mold. Freeze for 24 hours. Before serving, remove from mold and slice.

Serves 8 to 10

Chinese Almond Cookies

1 cup lard
1 cup shortening
1 3/4 cups sugar
2 eggs
2 teaspoons almond extract
1 teaspoon vanilla
4 1/2 cups unsifted all-purpose flour
1 teaspoon baking soda
2 teaspoons baking powder
3/4 cup finely chopped almonds

Preheat oven to 350 degrees. Grease two large cookie sheets and set aside. In large mixing bowl, with electric mixer at medium speed, cream lard, shortening, and sugar until light and fluffy. Add the eggs and extracts and continue beating until well mixed, scraping sides of bowl occasionally. In medium bowl, combine flour, baking powder, and baking soda. Gradually add dry ingredients to creamed mixture; continue beating just until well mixed. Add almonds. Dough will be dry and crumbly. Roll dough into 1-inch balls, place on greased cookie sheet, and press flat with fork. Bake at 350 degrees for 12 to 15 minutes.

Makes 5 dozen

The Cohen Building, built around 1865, bears the name of the family who lived and worked there through several generations. The three-story 10,000-square-foot brick building housed distilleries, breweries, pawn shops, and dry goods stores before being completely renovated in 1981. The building displays some important architecture of the early nineteenth century, and now houses one of Paducah's most popular eateries.

C. C. Cohen Restaurant & Bar inhabits the first two floors of the building, with offices and storage on the third floor. The first floor features a collection of stained glass and antiques, down to the oak shoe-shine chair at the front entrance. The main restaurant is on this floor, where the friendly staff serves up the food that made C. C. Cohen famous.

Appetizers include stuffed potato skins, one of the most popular items on the menu. Cohen's crab claws are also much in demand, featuring a half pound of gulf crab claws, dipped in batter and fried.

At lunch time many patrons order one of Cohen's classic burgers, and have to choose from no less than six different variations on the hamburger theme. The Cordon Bleu Burger has sliced ham, Swiss cheese, lettuce, onion and tomato, and the New Orleans Burger features Creole seasoning, mozzarella cheese, and the works. Soups and salads abound, offering everything from French Onion and Beer Cheese soup to the classic Greek or chef's salad.

C. C. Cohen
Restaurant & Bar

The dinner menu is extensive, featuring a variety of seafood and chicken entrées and C. C. Cohen's famous steaks, cut fresh daily and charbroiled to perfection. The King-Cut prime rib is a wonder to behold, and the blackened prime rib, rubbed in Cajun spices and cooked in an iron skillet, will satisfy the hungriest diner! For those watching their calories, C. C. Cohen has a special low-fat/no-fat menu with dynamite entrées such as chicken fettuccine or charbroiled red snapper.

The second floor is the banquet/private party room,

complete with bar, dance floor, and booth for a disc jockey. The second floor is a popular gathering place, and on Friday live blues bands play from around the South. On Saturday, restaurant owner Alan Raidt and his band, Alan Raidt and Friends, play downstairs. The music combines old and new acoustic tunes as well as some of Paducah's best blues. The band is featured on KET, Kentucky's educational television network.

For "good food, good fun, and good friends," C. C. Cohen's is the place to go!

C.C. Cohen
Restaurant & Bar

Proprietor: Alan Raidt.

Address: 103 Market House Square, Paducah, KY 42001.

Telephone: (502) 442-6391. Fax: (502) 442-3598.

Hours: Monday through Thursday, 11:00 a.m. to 9:00 p.m.; Friday and Saturday from 11:00 a.m. to 10:00 p.m.; closed Sunday. Entertainment starts at 10:00 p.m. Friday and Saturday.

Season: Open year round.

Seating: Reservations not necessary, but accepted.

Credit cards: Visa, MasterCard, American Express, and Discover.

Directions: From Interstate 24 take exit 4 east toward downtown Paducah (U.S. Highway 60). Stay on Highway 60 until Broadway. Turn left, and go two blocks to the corner of Broadway and 2nd (Market House Square) to C. C. Cohen.

C. C. Cohen's Pasta Salad

1 1/4 pounds (dry weight) mixed color rotini noodles
1 chopped green bell pepper
2 16-ounce cans green peas
1 large cucumber, chopped
1/2 cup sliced pepperoni, quartered
2 celery sticks, chopped
1/2 cup mayonnaise
2 cups ranch dressing
1/2 cup red wine vinegar
1 tablespoon basil
1 tablespoon oregano
1 tablespoon granulated garlic
1 tablespoon black pepper
1 tablespoon lemon pepper
1/2 cup olive oil
1 tablespoon lemon juice
1/2 cup sugar

Cook noodles until tender; let cool. Mix remaining ingredients with noodles and chill.

Serves 10 to 12

C. C. Cohen's French Onion Soup

6 medium yellow onions, coarsely chopped
1/2 gallon water
1 ounce au jus mix
1 ounce cream
1/2 teaspoon beef base
dash Kitchen Bouquet

Combine ingredients. Cook on medium heat until onions are clear, stirring frequently. To serve, top with Holland Rusk toast from your grocer's gourmet section. If unavailable, use unbuttered toast cut to the shape of the bowl.

Serves 8

C. C. Cohen's Muffalata Dressing

1/2 cup finely chopped green olives
1/2 cup finely chopped red onions
1 cup virgin olive oil
1 teaspoon red wine vinegar
1/2 teaspoon Creole seasoning
1/2 teaspoon basil
1/2 teaspoon chopped garlic

Mix olives and red onions. Add olive oil and blend to rich consistency. Add vinegar and spices.

Makes 12 servings of dressing

Try this suggestion for a Muffalata sandwich: stack thinly sliced turkey, ham, mozzarella cheese, and pepperoni in pan and steam. Slather dressing on top. Serve on French loaf cut in half or in pita pocket bread.

C. C. Cohen's B–B–Q Ribs

30 pounds baby back ribs, about 1/5 pounds per rack

Baste:
1 quart beer
1 tablespoon red vinegar
2 tablespoons liquid smoke

Sauce:
1/2 cup white vinegar
1/2 gallon Bullseye barbecue sauce
12 ounces beer
1 tablespoon liquid smoke
1 teaspoon red vinegar

Brown ribs on grill bone side down first, then flip to meat side when blood rises. Rub baste on ribs as they are browning. Put a rack or screen (such as a broiler screen) in the bottom of a deep hotel-sized pan and place ribs on top. Add leftover baste and add more if needed to fill to top of screen line. Mix sauce and pour over ribs, covering them. Cover pan with foil, tightly. Cook in a large oven at 250 to 275 degrees for 5 hours.

Serves 20

The secret is to keep a tight seal with the foil to let the ribs boil in the pan.

C. C. Cohen's Taco Spice and Taco Beef

Taco beef spice:
1 cup cumin
1/2 cup granulated garlic
1/4 cup salt
1/4 cup black pepper
1/4 cup chili powder

Taco beef:
2 pounds ground beef
2 large onions, chopped
1 large green bell pepper, chopped
2 pints water
2 cans hot chili beans
1 1/2 cups taco beef spice (use above recipe)

Brown beef, drain fat, add remaining ingredients, and simmer 45 minutes.

Serves 6 to 8

On rainy days, this different-tasting taco filling should appease your family's south-of-the-border demands!

Country Cupboard made its name serving good, old-fashioned country cooking, and lots of it. A bright, open restaurant with two dining rooms, it seats 135 people. All that space is needed, too, especially on weekends, when locals and visitors to the area want to enjoy a delicious meal at reasonable prices.

Country Cupboard is best known for its sumptuous buffets, offered at breakfast on Saturday and Sunday, and at lunch and dinner throughout the week. A full menu is also provided for all three meals. Come early for breakfast and choose eggs prepared to order with home fries or hash browns, omelets, cereal, fruit, pastries, hotcakes, or biscuits and gravy, or cruise by the buffet bar to see the many choices available there.

Lunch pulls in a big crowd, and deservedly so. Over 19 different kinds of sandwiches are on the menu, and 7 different hamburgers. Those in the mood for a salad have no less a difficult choice. The all-you-can-eat salad bar is always open at lunch, where diners can create their own salads from the delicious fruits and vegetables that are provided there. Five additional salads are offered on the menu as well, for those who prefer the cook to do all the work!

The dinner buffet is a sight to behold. A full salad bar is offered, and the hot food bar presents such a myriad of choices that customers are forced to keep coming back for more! Try the fried pork chops, shrimp, and clams, or load your plate high with crispy fried chicken. The pulled pork barbecue is tempting to many, as is the fried catfish. And the Southern-style vegetables! A variety of greens, corn, beets, Kentucky-style green beans, potatoes, and more are offered every night. And of course, hush puppies and rolls are available to complement the dinners.

Country Cupboard

If that weren't enough, the dinner buffet includes a trip to the dessert bar. A number of different kinds of pies such as lemon meringue, chess, and pecan are offered, as are fruit cobblers and creamy puddings. Just the thing to cap off a good meal, along with a cup of freshly brewed hot coffee!

Those who wish to order dinner from the menu choose between catfish platters, ribeye steaks, marinated chicken breast, shrimp, honey-baked ham, or sirloin beef tips. All kinds of sandwiches and salads are available, as are extras like beer-battered onion rings, deep-fried mushrooms, tater tots, hot wings and broasted potatoes.

Tour groups are welcome at Country Cupboard, and the establishment has no difficultly seating large groups of people, although it is is best to call ahead so seating preparations can be made in advance. Proprietor Carmen Rhew is usually at the door to greet customers with a smile, and the waitresses are friendly and efficient. A true West Kentucky experience!

COUNTRY CUPBOARD

Proprietors: Carmen Rhew, Phyllis and Wayne Browning.

Address: U.S. Highway 62 West, Eddyville, KY 42038.

Telephone: (502) 388-5178.

Hours: Breakfast Monday through Friday, 7:00 a.m. to 10:30 a.m. Saturday and Sunday breakfast buffet from 7:00 a.m. to 11:00 a.m. Lunch 10:30 a.m. to 4:00 p.m. Monday through Friday, 11:00 a.m. to 4:00 p.m. Saturday and Sunday. Dinner Monday through Thursday 4:00 p.m. to 8:00 p.m., Friday through Saturday 4:00 p.m. to 9:00 p.m., Sunday from 11:00 a.m. to 8:00 p.m.

Season: Open all year.

Seating: Reservations suggested. Reservations for large groups necessary.

Credit cards: Not accepted.

Directions: At the Eddyville stoplight on U.S. Highway 62 West, across from the West Kentucky Factory Outlet Mall.

Chess Pie

2 cups sugar
1 teaspoon vanilla
1 cup evaporated milk
2/3 stick butter
1 tablespoon plain flour
1 tablespoon cornmeal
dash salt
3 eggs
1 unbaked 9-inch pie shell

Mix all ingredients together and pour into pie shell. Bake at 350 degrees for 45 minutes.

Serves 8

Chocolate Chip Pie

1/2 cup plain flour
1 cup sugar
1 stick butter
2 eggs
1 teaspoon vanilla
1 cup coarsely chopped pecans
1 cup chocolate chips
1 unbaked pie shell

Mix all ingredients together and pour into pie shell. Bake at 350 degrees for 45 minutes.

Serves 8

Japanese Fruit Pie

1 teaspoon vanilla
1 1/2 cups sugar
3 eggs
1 stick butter
1 tablespoon vinegar
1/2 cup raisins
1 cup coconut
1/2 cup coarsely chopped pecans
1 unbaked 9-inch pie shell

Mix all ingredients together and pour into pie shell. Bake at 350 degrees for 45 minutes.

Serves 8

Fudge Brownie Pudding

1 cup self-rising flour
3/4 cup sugar
2 tablespoons cocoa
2 tablespoons butter
1 teaspoon vanilla
1/2 cup milk
1 cup sugar
2 tablespoons cocoa
pinch salt
1 1/2 cups hot water

Mix together the first six ingredients and pour into greased brownie pan. Mix remaining sugar, cocoa, and salt, and sprinkle mixture over the batter in the pan (do not mix). Pour hot water over the mixture in the pan. Bake at 350 degrees for 45 minutes or until toothpick inserted in center comes out clean.

Serves 8

Fudge Pie

3 tablespoons cocoa
3/4 stick butter
2 cups sugar
3 1/2 tablespoons plain flour
pinch salt
1 teaspoon vanilla
1/2 cup milk
3 eggs, beaten
1 unbaked 9-inch pie shell

Melt butter and stir in cocoa. Mix together sugar, flour, and salt. Add vanilla, milk, and eggs. Mix well and pour into pie shell. Bake at 350 degrees for 45 minutes.

Serves 8

In operation for over thirty years, The Cumberland House Restaurant is known in West Kentucky as the place to eat for an extraordinary seafood buffet. With its seaside decor, relaxing atmosphere, and congenial hosts Patsy and Paul Smith, patrons return again and again to enjoy the sumptuous repast.

Diners who choose the buffet are faced with over fifty delicious choices to fill their plates, including frog legs, peel & eat shrimp, clams, scallops, baked salmon, and steaming hot crab legs. Also included in the buffet are the much-acclaimed house accompaniments: red beans and rice, hush puppies, cabbage Creole, sautéed mushrooms, and seafood stir fry. Those with larger appetites can also order lobster tail, ribeye steak, fillet mignon, or prime rib to accompany the buffet. Catfish lovers are offered an all-you-can-eat catfish dinner that includes potatoes, white beans, hush puppies, and slaw.

The menu features traditional fare that is as appetizing as the seafood buffet. Prime rib, steaks, and chicken are freshly cut and grilled nightly by Patsy and Paul's son and head chef, Michael Smith. A soup & salad bar is available for those with lighter appetites, and a seafood salad bar includes shrimp, crab salad, smoked oysters, baked salmon, and all the offerings of the soup & salad bar.

The Cumberland House Restaurant

The Cumberland House welcomes children, greeting them at the door with Captain Jack, a life-size riverboat captain mannequin (featuring the voice of Paul Smith, who pretends to be a customer in the gift shop so he can watch the delighted reactions of his little guests). A special menu is provided for children with hamburgers, corn dogs, and other items children love. The seafood buffet is available at a reduced price for children under 12.

Patsy arrives each morning at six o'clock to bake her famous homemade bread, and to whip up some strawberry and honey butter and various specialties that will be featured in the restaurant that night. In addition to the sumptuous buffet, Patsy prepares delicious homemade desserts for the dessert bar.

Homemade cheesecakes, cakes, chess bars, and the famous Cumberland House Scalloped Pineapple are sure to tempt the sweet tooth of any diner.

The Cumberland House opens nightly during the summer and on weekends during the off-season. Reservations are preferred in summer months, and special dining rooms are available for small parties.

The Cumberland House Restaurant

Proprietors: Patsy and Paul Smith.

Address: 5017 U.S. Highway 62 West, Kuttawa, KY 42055.

Telephone: (502) 388-7722.

Hours: The restaurant opens at 5:00 p.m. for dinner.

Season: March through Memorial Day, open Thursday through Sunday. From Memorial Day through Labor Day, open nightly. From Labor Day through December, open Thursday through Saturday. Closed mid-December through February.

Seating: Reservations suggested during the summer season.

Credit cards: Visa, MasterCard, American Express, and Discover.

Directions: From exit 40 off Interstate 24 (the Eddyville/Kuttawa exit), two miles west on U.S. 62 West.

Fish Parmesan

1 pound cod fish fillets
1 tablespoon chopped onion
1 cup sour cream
1/4 cup Parmesan cheese
2 tablespoons lemon juice
1/2 teaspoon salt
1/4 teaspoon ground pepper
dash hot pepper sauce
dash paprika
chopped parsley for garnish

Place fillets in single layer in a well-greased baking dish. Combine all remaining ingredients except paprika and parsley. Sprinkle with paprika and bake at 350 degrees for 20 to 25 minutes. Sprinkle with parsley.

Serves 2 to 3

The fillets can also be cooked on the grill, by wrapping in foil and keeping the foil closed until done. Delicious also with other types of fish.

Patsy's Veggie Bites

1 8-ounce package refrigerated crescent rolls
1 egg, beaten
1 8-ounce package cream cheese
1 cup mayonnaise
1/2 1-ounce envelope ranch dressing mix
3/4 cup shredded cheese
1/2 cup chopped broccoli
1/2 cup chopped cauliflower
1/2 cup chopped mushrooms
1/2 cup chopped green peppers
1/2 cup chopped fresh tomatoes

Unroll crescent rolls and place in bottom of ungreased 15 x 10 x 1 inch jelly roll pan. Pinch edges to seal. Brush dough with beaten egg. Bake at 375 degrees for 10 to 12 minutes until brown. Cool completely. Combine cream cheese, mayonnaise, and ranch mix and spread mixture over cooled crust. Sprinkle with vegetables and shredded cheese. Chill. Cut into squares.

Makes about 4 dozen

Add your favorite vegetables to make this dish special!

Hot Cabbage Creole

1 1/2 heads cabbage, chopped
1 1/2 tablespoons salt
1/2 tablespoon black pepper
1/4 teaspoon cayenne pepper
3 large ripe tomatoes, quartered
2 quarts tomato sauce
2 green peppers, sliced
1 large purple onion, chopped
1/2 cup vinegar
3/4 cup brown sugar
1/2 pound uncooked bacon, chopped

Put all ingredients into large pot on top of stove and cook on medium heat, stirring occasionally until cabbage is tender.

Serves 10 to 12

Cumberland House Scalloped Pineapple

4 cups bread cubes
20 ounces canned pineapple chunks
3 eggs, beaten
2 cups sugar
3/4 cup liquid margarine

Layer bread cubes into baking dish sprayed with non-stick cooking spray. Drain juice from pineapple chunks , reserving juice, and layer chunks over bread cubes. Mix beaten eggs, sugar, liquid margarine, and pineapple juice together and pour over pineapple. Bake at 350 degrees about 20 minutes or until it gets hot and starts to brown.

Serves 8 to 10

Patsy suggests using day-old homemade bread for best results. This Cumberland House specialty is famous through-out West Kentucky and parts beyond!

Fudge Brownie Cake

1 stick margarine
2 cups sugar
5 eggs
1/2 cup cocoa
1 cup self-rising flour
pinch salt
1/2 cup pecans, chopped
2 teaspoons vanilla

Combine sugar and margarine, stirring with a large spoon (do not use a mixer). Stir until creamed. Mix in eggs, cocoa, flour, salt, nuts, and vanilla. Bake in a well-greased and floured 8 x 11 1/2 inch pan or Pyrex dish at 350 degrees for about 20 minutes. The brownie should be soft in the center but not raw.

Fudge Brownie Cake Icing

1 pound powdered sugar
1/2 cup cocoa
1 stick margarine
2 teaspoons vanilla
1/4 cup milk

Cream all ingredients together and spread over warm cake.

DiFabio's Casapela is a family-owned and -operated Italian restaurant. Peter DiFabio handles the business side of the restaurant and oversees kitchen production. His wife Laura supervises food preparation and lovingly prepares all of the desserts herself. Their daughters Sarah and Caitlind help with hostessing duties, wait tables, and even lend a hand washing dishes. The name Casapela is derived from the first two letters of each name: Caitlind, Sarah, Peter, and Laura.

Together Peter and Laura have over thirty-five years of experience in the restaurant business. Active home entertainers, they were repeatedly urged by their friends to open their own restaurant, and DiFabio's Casapela is the result. Guests in the restaurant are treated as guests are in the DiFabio home.

Needless to say, the combination of delicious, home-made Italian food and gracious hospitality has proven highly successful. DiFabio's was voted Best All Around Restaurant by the *Madisonville Messenger*'s People's Choice in 1996.

Much-loved Italian dishes are prepared to perfection at DiFabio's. A host of *antipasti* are offered to begin the meal, including Artichoke Fritters, Baked Stuffed Mushroom Caps, and Sausage en Croute. All dinner entrées are served with crunchy Italian salads and soft, garlicky bread sticks warm from the oven. The specialties of the house include Chicken Piccata or Parmigiana, Lasagna, Manicotti, and Tortellini Alfredo.

DiFabio's Casapela

The veal and shrimp specials of the day are always popular choices with diners.

Creative people enjoy the "choose-your-own" aspect of the many pasta dishes offered. Diners choose their favorite sauce — everything from tomato sauce with meatballs to pesto, alfredo, and marinara is offered — and then decide which pasta will best complement their choice. Delectable and light angel hair, traditional spaghetti or linguine, and hearty fettuccine are all available.

The famous "Casapela Bus Trip" is on the menu every night, and provides a sampling for those who want a taste of it all. The plate features three items that change nightly, and typically includes two pasta dishes, one with a white sauce and one with a red, and a meat entrée. Dessert is also included, and all for a fixed price. It is evident the tempting *dolci* featured at DiFabio's are painstakingly prepared from family recipes. Italian cheesecake, spumoni ice cream, canoli and tiramisù all provide a memorable end to a meal. A wide variety of soups, salads, pasta, and sandwiches are available at lunch, as are several specials.

Try DiFabio's Casapela for the next best thing to a trip to Rome!

Proprietors: Peter and Laura DiFabio.

Address: 17 West Center Street, Madisonville, KY 42431.

Telephone: (502) 825-1900.

Hours: Lunch, 11:00 a.m. to 2:00 p.m. Tuesday through Friday; dinner, 5:00 p.m. to 9:00 p.m. Tuesday through Thursday, 5:00 p.m. to 10:00 p.m. Friday and Saturday. Closed Sunday and Monday.

Season: Open all year.

Seating: Reservations recommended on weekends. Small private banquet room available.

Credit cards: Visa and MasterCard.

Directions: From Pennyrile Parkway take exit 42 heading west. Turn left (south) on Main Street and then right on Center Street at the courthouse. Located on the right within the first block.

Minestrone Soup

1/2 pound bacon
1/2 pound Italian sausage
1/2 cup diced onion
1/2 cup diced green pepper
1 1/2 tablespoons minced garlic
1 tablespoon Italian parsley, chopped
4 quarts beef broth
1 1/2 quarts tomato sauce
1/2 tablespoon garlic powder
1 tablespoon oregano
1 tablespoon basil
1/2 tablespoon thyme
1/2 tablespoon crushed fennel
1/2 teaspoon crushed red pepper
4 ounces frozen spinach
13 ounces kidney beans
1 1/4 cups mixed vegetables, fresh or frozen
(zucchini, summer squash, carrots, green beans, etc.)
1 1/4 cups short noodle pasta of choice
croutons and Parmesan cheese for garnish

Dice and sauté bacon until almost crisp. Drain. Remove casing from sausage, dice, and sauté with bacon until done. Add onion and pepper and sauté until tender. Add garlic and parsley and cook 1 minute. Then add broth, tomato sauce, garlic powder, oregano, basil, thyme, fennel, and red pepper. Allow to come to a boil, then add spinach, beans, and vegetables. Simmer for about 30 minutes. Add pasta and allow to simmer another 30 minutes. The soup is ready to serve when the pasta is tender. Garnish with croutons and Parmesan cheese.

Makes 9 to 10 quarts, (about 40 8-ounce servings)

Pesto Salmon

1 tablespoon butter
3 ounces white wine
1 clove garlic, minced
8 ounces fresh Atlantic salmon fillet
1 teaspoon pesto (prepared)

Melt butter in sauté pan. Add wine, garlic, and salmon fillet. Reduce by one-third. Cover and simmer until salmon is done, approximately 10 minutes. Cooking time will vary due to thickness of fillet. Brush cooked fillet with pesto.

Serves 1

Italian Cheesecake

1 pound ricotta cheese
1 pound cream cheese
1 1/2 cups sugar
4 eggs
3 tablespoons cornstarch
3 tablespoons flour
1 teaspoon vanilla extract
grated peel from one lemon
juice from one lemon
2 cups sour cream
1/2 cup melted butter

Put both cheeses and sugar in mixing bowl and combine. Add eggs, cornstarch, flour, vanilla, lemon peel, and lemon juice. Mix well. Add sour cream and butter, and mix until smooth.

Put in greased springform pan and bake for 1 hour at 325 degrees. Turn off oven and leave in oven for 1 1/2 hours. Refrigerate 8 hours before serving.

Serves 10

Creamy Garlic Sauce

3 tablespoons minced garlic
6 ounces butter
1/2 cup all-purpose flour
1/2 cup dry white wine
1/2 cup water
2 quarts heavy cream
1/2 teaspoon ground white pepper
salt as needed

Sauté garlic in butter until softened. Whisk in flour and cook over medium heat 3 to 4 minutes. Do not brown. Add wine, water, cream, salt, and pepper. Mix well. Bring to simmer and cook 15 minutes.

Serves 12

This is a versatile base sauce that is great when tossed with fresh cooked pasta and cooked seafood such as scallops, shrimp, or salmon. Add fresh basil or sun-dried tomatoes for extra color and flavor.

CocoLoco Bars

1 cup butter (not margarine)
1/2 cup unsweetened cocoa
2 large eggs
1/2 cup sugar
2 teaspoons vanilla extract
2 cups unsweetened coconut
1 quart (4 cups) graham cracker crumbs
1/2 cup chopped walnuts
1 pound box confectioner's sugar
1/2 cup soft butter
1/3 cup milk
1/2 cup instant vanilla pudding mix
1 pound chocolate chips
2 tablespoons butter
1 cup milk

Combine first 4 ingredients in top of double boiler until it reaches custard consistency. Remove from heat and add vanilla. Combine coconut, crumbs, and nuts, then add to cocoa mixture. Press into bottom of 12 x 18 inch greased pan. With a high-speed mixer, mix confectioner's sugar, soft butter, 1/3 cup milk, and pudding mix. Beat until smooth and fluffy, then spread over crumb mixture. In double boiler, stirring constantly, heat chips, butter, and 1 cup milk until melted and smooth. Spread over crumbs and pudding in pan. Refrigerate about 1 hour. Cut into squares.

Makes 24 large bars or 48 small ones

Very popular with chocolate lovers!

The story behind Historic Oldtown Restaurant would make for a very entertaining movie. The Holmes family of Marshall County, the current owners, have been faithful to the past, and throughout the restaurant they pay tribute to the colorful history of the building.

Oldtown was a stagecoach stop in 1847, where horses and travelers were fed and watered, and riders could find a drink, a card game, and an occasional gunfight. Ten years later, it had the distinction of becoming the first establishment in West Kentucky to obtain a tavern license. Local legend has it that during the Battle of Paducah in 1864 General Grant's forces seized and utilized Oldtown as part of the Union encampment, due to its close proximity to Fort Anderson, which was located where the Executive Inn now stands.

Around the turn of the century, Oldtown became famous as a house of ill repute, and it is said that the madam of the place, Carolina, now haunts Oldtown as a benevolent ghost. With the onset of Prohibition, Oldtown was converted into a speakeasy, complete with a plant upstairs where gin was manufactured in a bathtub, then lowered through a secret opening to the tavern below. During the 1930s it became J&S Tavern, a popular eatery, and in 1994 became Historic Oldtown Restaurant, where patrons can enjoy a taste of the Old West in an environment reminiscent of yesteryear.

Historic Oldtown Restaurant

Famous for its baby back ribs and succulent steaks, Oldtown prides itself on serving USDA beef that is fresh, never frozen, and cooked over a charcoal hearth fired with select hardwoods. The Oldtown Traveler's Filet Mignon and the Gambler's Del Monico Steak are grilled to order, and a delicious surf and turf combination is offered in the Stagecoach Petite Filet with Jumbo Shrimp.

Fresh seafood dishes are on the menu daily, including the catch of the day, Seafood Kabob Orleans, and Shrimp Scampi Louisianne. The Chicken Marsala is a popular menu item, as is the Fettuccine Alfredo. The soup of the day is prepared fresh daily, and is accompanied by a pot of bread, baked fresh every morning and served with various flavored butters. Desserts are absolutely luscious, and the homemade cheesecake and chocolate cheesecake mousse are sure to tempt.

A wide variety of sandwiches, burgers, soups and salads is available for lunch, and Happy Hour from 4:00 to 6:00 each day is a popular time to catch up with friends. Stop by Historic Oldtown Restaurant for a bit of local history and a delightful dining experience!

Proprietor: Historic Oldtown Restaurant, Inc.

Address: 701 Park Avenue, Paducah, KY 42001.

Telephone: (502) 442-9616.

Hours: Lunch from 11:00 a.m. to 2:00 p.m.; Happy Hour from 4:00 p.m. to 6:00 p.m.; dinner from 5:00 p.m. until closing. Closed Sunday and Monday.

Season: Open year round.

Seating: Reservations recommended.

Credit cards: Visa, MasterCard, American Express, Discover, and Diner's Club.

Directions: Two blocks northwest of the Executive Inn on Park Avenue. From Kentucky Oaks Mall: go east until 7th Street, turn left, and travel one block. Historic Oldtown Restaurant is on the corner of 7th and Park.

Beer Batter

2 cups all-purpose flour
4 eggs
4 12-ounce bottles dark beer

Mix all ingredients together. Dip chosen items in batter and deep fry.

Makes 1 batch

This batter is used at Oldtown for their Legendary Cheese Sticks. Excellent on shrimp, chicken strips, and onion blossoms.

Beefy Onion Soup

2 to 3 pounds beef
2 quarts beef broth
6 large onions, thinly sliced
2 tablespoons basil
1 tablespoon tarragon
2 teaspoons garlic powder
1/2 cup Kitchen Bouquet
salt and pepper to taste

Grill meat over charcoal until done and cut into bite-size pieces. Bring beef broth to a boil and reduce to simmer. Add meat, onions, and remaining ingredients. Simmer for 1 hour or until onions are tender.

Makes 1 gallon

Stuffed Mushroom Caps

2 pounds whole hog sausage
2 tablespoons garlic powder
1 tablespoon onion powder
1/4 cup dry Italian seasoning
1 teaspoon crushed red pepper
1 cup bread crumbs
1/4 cup grated Parmesan cheese
2 dozen large mushrooms

Mix all ingredients except mushrooms together and set aside. Rinse mushrooms and pull stems out. Slice a little off of the top of the mushroom so it will sit flat on a tray. Take sausage mixture and stuff mushrooms so the mixture stands 3/4 inch above the cap. Bake at 350 degrees for 10 minutes. After baking, sprinkle Parmesan cheese on top of sausage and return to oven until cheese starts to melt.

Makes 2 dozen

Cajun Prime Rib

1 4-bone prime rib (about 10 pounds)
1/4 cup black pepper
1/4 cup garlic powder
1/4 cup salt
1 tablespoon white pepper
2 tablespoons whole fennel seed
2 teaspoons cayenne pepper
2 medium onions, thinly sliced

Mix all spices together. Cut the fat cap away from the meat but do not cut off. Rub all the seasonings into meat. Lay all the onions on top of seasonings. Pull fat cap back up and around meat and secure into place. Refrigerate for 24 hours. Bake at 350 degrees for 5 hours. This amount of cooking will produce a prime rib that is medium rare to medium.

Serves 10

Oldtown Cheesecake

2 cups ground vanilla wafers (about 60 wafers)
8 tablespoons (1 stick) melted butter
2 pounds cream cheese
1 1/2 cups sugar
3 tablespoons all-purpose flour
1/4 teaspoon salt
4 large eggs
1/4 cup whipping cream
1 teaspoon vanilla extract
strawberries for garnish

Combine vanilla wafers and melted butter; blend well. Generously butter a 9-inch springform pan on sides and bottom. Press crumbs on sides and bottom of pan, making a thin layer. Beat cream cheese until it is perfectly smooth. Combine sugar, flour, and salt, and add this mixture to cheese. Add eggs, one at a time, beating well. Add the cream and vanilla, mixing thoroughly. Spoon mixture into buttered pan. The pan should be more than 3/4 full. Bake in preheated 300-degree oven on middle shelf for 1 hour.

Turn off heat and leave cake in oven with door open for 15 to 20 minutes. Allow cake to cool completely at room temperature. Remove cake from pan and refrigerate. Garnish with strawberries.

Serves 10

Situated in downtown Paducah in the graceful old Ritz Hotel, the House of Grace is a delightful place to stop and have lunch during the week. Building on the fine dining traditions set by Curtis Grace at the famous Ninth Street House, son Tim Grace has established a restaurant where devoted patrons of exceptionally good food can indulge their gourmet tastes.

The Grace family classic, California Chicken Salad, is a bestseller at the House of Grace. A delicious concoction of shredded chicken, sliced green grapes, toasted almonds, and a special curry dressing, this hearty salad has been famous in Paducah for years. The delicious House of Grace iced tea, a sweetened tea flavored with fruit juice and made from a secret recipe, is served by the gallons at lunch each day.

Those who wish to try something other than the famed California Chicken Salad might go with Curtis' Chicken Salad or the Pantry Special, featuring homemade toast topped with Swiss cheese, lettuce, turkey, Pantry dressing, tomato, and hard-boiled eggs. All of the dressings served at the House of Grace are homemade, as is the flavorful white bread used for the sandwiches. Sliced baked ham, tuna salad, pimiento cheese, and chicken salad sandwiches are all prepared fresh each morning using homemade spreads and that tasty, oven-fresh bread.

The luncheon buffet offers a number of dishes that are varied according to the whim

House of Grace

of the chef. A cold pasta salad, hot casserole dish, several vegetables, and an entrée are presented each day in the buffet. The homemade strawberry shortcake is offered by popular demand and is another House of Grace bestseller. Homemade pies such as Key Lime and Pecan also appear on the dessert menu and are rotated with other delights to provide different choices.

The House of Grace is open for lunch only, so aficionados make certain to carve time in their busy daily schedules to stop by and sample the day's offerings. The food can be ordered to go, and the carry-out side of the restaurant is open until 4:00 for those who want to order something to bring home for an early supper.

The floor-to-ceiling windows at the House of Grace

provide a view of the downtown scene, and the chic burgundy wallpaper and window valances add a sophisticated touch. The antiques placed throughout the high-ceilinged room complement the charming bistro atmosphere.

Visit the House of Grace, where the Grace family's tradition of fine gourmet dining continues to please.

Proprietor: Tim Grace.

Address: 2201 Broadway, Paducah, KY 42001. In the Ritz Hotel, ground floor.

Telephone: (502) 443-5356.

Hours: Open 11:00 a.m. to 3: 00 p.m. Monday through Friday. Carry-out available until 4:00 p.m.

Season: Open all year.

Seating: No reservations necessary.

Credit cards: Visa and Mastercard.

Directions: From Interstate 24, take exit 4 (U.S. Highway 60 North) to 22nd and Broadway.

Cucumber Soup

1 cup sour cream
1 cucumber, peeled, seeded, and sliced
1/4 teaspoon dry mustard
1 cup chicken broth
1 tablespoon snipped chives or green onion
salt and pepper to taste

Put all ingredients into a blender and blend only until cucumber is finely chopped, not smooth. Chill and serve. Garnish with a sprinkle of dill or chives if desired.

Serves 2 to 4

California Chicken Salad

1/2 cup butter
2 cups mayonnaise
1/4 cup parsley, minced
1/2 teaspoon curry powder
1/4 teaspoon garlic, minced
pinch of marjoram
salt and pepper to taste
4 cups cooked chicken breasts, shredded (about 4 small breasts)
2 cups seedless green grapes, sliced
1/2 cup toasted, slivered almonds
lettuce leaves

Melt butter in saucepan. Cool to room temperature. In a bowl, gently stir the butter into mayonnaise, parsley, curry powder, garlic, marjoram, salt, and pepper. In a large bowl, combine chicken, grapes, and almonds. Arrange this mixture on lettuce leaves. Spoon dressing on top and sprinkle with paprika.

Serves 4

Hot Turkey Casserole

1 to 1 1/2 cups cooked turkey, chopped
1/2 cup Kraft mayonnaise
1/2 can cream of chicken soup
1/2 can cream of mushroom soup
2 chopped hard-boiled eggs
1/2 cup toasted sliced almonds
1/2 teaspoon minced onion
1 can water chestnuts, drained
1/3 cup bread crumbs

Mix all ingredients except bread crumbs thoroughly. Place in greased casserole and top with crumbs. Bake at 350 degrees for 20 minutes.

Serves 6

Vegetable Pie

1 pound fresh mushrooms, sliced
1 onion, sliced
2 zucchini or yellow squash, sliced
1 green pepper, sliced
3 or 4 tablespoons butter
1 teaspoon salt
1/4 teaspoon black pepper
dash garlic salt
1 10-inch pie shell, pre-baked at 325 degrees for 20 minutes
1 tomato, sliced
1 cup mayonnaise
1 cup mozzarella cheese, grated

Sauté vegetables in butter until crisp but not soft. Drain well and add seasonings. Place tomato slices in bottom of pre-baked pie shell. Add vegetables. Mix mayonnaise and cheese and spread mixture over vegetables. Bake uncovered at 325 degrees for 45 minutes to 1 hour.

Serves 6

Party Chicken Salad

6 ounces lemon gelatin
2 cups boiling water
2 cups cream, whipped
1 8-ounce package cream cheese
1 1/2 cups chopped celery
1 cup stuffed olives, sliced

Dissolve lemon gelatin in boiling water. Cool. When it reaches the consistency of egg whites, fold in whipped cream and cream cheese that has been softened with a little milk. Add remaining ingredients. Fold together gently and pour into a 9 x 12 inch pan that has been coated with mayonnaise. Chill and cut into squares.

Topping:
3 - 4 cups chicken or turkey, diced
1 pint Hellmann's mayonnaise
1 tablespoon, chopped
1 1/2 tablespoons lemon juice

Mix all ingredients together. Place squares of gelatin mixture on lettuce leaves. Spoon topping on individual servings. Garnish with tomato wedges, avocado slices, or both.

Serves 12 to 15

Kentucky State Resort Park Lodges

Lake Barkley State Resort Park

Lake Barkley State Resort Park near Cadiz, in Trigg County, is truly a work of art. The architects and designers of this timbered recreational haven have blended the rustic and ancient landscape of rural Kentucky with the comfortable conveniences of our modern times.

One must begin at the beautiful lodge. Sitting majestically on a narrow peninsula leading out into the waters of Lake Barkley, this timbered edifice of redwood and glass offers first-class accommodations with a breathtaking view. In addition to 120 rooms and four lodge suites, the main hotel also sports a large swimming pool, gift shop, recreational rooms, coffee shop, and, perhaps most spectacularly, a spacious dining hall with room for over 300 people. Whether in summer when sailboats fill the horizon or in winter when the huge stone fireplace crackles with a cozy fire, dining is the high point of anyone's visit.

One might be tempted to simply become ensconced in the spacious and lovely confines of the lodge. But don't overlook the other fine facilities.

There are 13 cottages for rent, endless hiking trails, horseback riding, playgrounds, shuffleboard, tennis courts, trapshooting, and a 4,800-foot lighted airstrip for aviation buffs. The 18-hole Boots Randolph Golf Course, with its well-stocked pro shop, is one of the finest in the state.

Lake Barkley Fitness Center is not to be missed by those who enjoy keeping in top physical condition, while having fun at the same time. Located next to the lodge, the center offers Nautilus exercise equipment, a jacuzzi, a sauna and steam rooms, a tanning bed, racquetball courts, and a large aerobic dance room.

As one can quickly see, Lake Barkley State Resort Park has a lot to offer, and all tastefully arranged in the middle of 3,600 acres of some of West Kentucky's most scenic woodland.

Barkley Bar-B-Q Sauce

1/2 cup onions, finely chopped
vegetable oil
2 quarts catsup, tomato sauce, or tomato puree
3 ounces Worcestershire sauce
1/3 small bottle Tabasco sauce
1/2 pound brown sugar
1/4 cup lemon juice
1 tablespoon liquid smoke
1 cup apple cider vinegar
poultry, beef, or pork

Saute onions in small amount of vegetable oil. Add catsup, Worcestershire sauce, Tabasco, sugar, lemon juice, liquid smoke, and vinegar, and mix well. Simmer approximately 30 minutes, stirring frequently. Season meat and partially cook one half of cooking time. Apply sauce and finish cooking meat slowly. Baste several times with sauce during final cooking phase.

<u>Proprietor</u>: The Commonwealth of Kentucky.

<u>Address:</u> Lake Barkley State Resort Park, Box 790, Cadiz, KY 42211-0790.

<u>Telephone</u>: (502) 924-1131. Toll-free: 1-800-255-PARK or 1-800-325-1708.

<u>Hours</u>: Dining room serves breakfast from 7:00 a.m. to 10:30 a.m.; lunch, 11:30 a.m. to 2:30 p.m.; dinner, 5:30 p.m. to 9:00 p.m. Overnight guests check in after 4:00 p.m.; checkout time is 11:00 a.m. in cottages, noon in lodge.

<u>Season</u>: Open year round.

<u>Seating</u>: Reservations not necessary for dining.

<u>Credit cards</u>: American Express, Visa, MasterCard, and Discover.

<u>Directions</u>: Park entrance is 7 miles west of Cadiz on U.S. Highway 68.

Perched at the northern end of the West Kentucky vacation area is one of the state's finest recreational complexes, welcoming southbound travelers into the friendly lands of Barkley and Kentucky lakes. It is, of course, Kentucky Dam Village State Resort Park. The impoundment of the Tennessee River, which created Kentucky Lake, begins here. Kentucky Dam, completed in 1945 and adjacent to the park, is a striking tourist attraction in its own right.

Like so many other state resort parks in Kentucky, the showplace of Kentucky Dam State Resort Park is its main lodge, the Village Inn. This modern lodge, completed in 1962, sits high upon a hill overlooking the wide and scenic beginnings of Kentucky Lake. There are 72 rooms in the Village Inn, 14 rooms in the Village Green Inn, and one-, two-, and three-bedroom detached cottages available for overnight accommodations.

The 1,200-acre park reaches below the dam into the old Gilbertsville area, where one can find 221 state-supported campsites, each with water and electrical hookups and grills. A marina near the picnic area, which provides the largest docking facility in Kentucky's park system, is especially popular with sailboaters who find in this part of the lake some of the best freshwater sailing anywhere.

The 18-hole Village Green golf course is within easy

Kentucky Dam Village State Resort Park

walking distance of the lodge and is open all year. Other facilities include bicycle rentals, horseback riding, tennis, hiking trails, and swimming, both at the sparkling pool located at the lodge and the spacious sandy beach, within easy walking distance from the Village Inn. Gift shops offer handmade Kentucky items, and groceries are sold at the boat dock. During the summer months, there is live entertainment at the park presented by talented local groups.

Perhaps one of the most popular activities at Kentucky Dam Village State Resort Park is fishing. The marina provides boat rentals, as well as a complete line of fishing services, for those who like to take advantage of this bountiful feeding ground of crappie, bass, perch, and catfish.

Aviators can fly into the park and land on the 4,000-foot lighted airstrip. Air camping facilities (showers, bathrooms, and tent sites) are located by the strip for those hearty souls who want to fly in and camp overnight.

Kentucky Dam Village is a relaxing spot to enjoy for a day, overnight, or an entire vacation!

Kentucky State Parks

"the nation's finest"

Proprietor: Commonwealth of Kentucky.

Address: Kentucky Dam Village State Resort Park, P.O. Box 69, Gilbertsville, KY 42022-0069.

Telephone: (502) 362-4271. Toll-free: 1-800-255-PARK or 1-800-325-0146.

Hours: Dining room serves breakfast from 7:00 a.m. to 10:30 a.m.; lunch, 11:30 a.m. to 2:30 p.m.; dinner, 5:30 p.m. to 9:00 p.m. Overnight guests check in after 4:00 p.m.; checkout time is 11:00 a.m. cottages, noon in lodge.

Season: Open year round.

Seating: Reservations not necessary for dining.

Credit cards: American Express, Visa, MasterCard, and Discover.

Directions: Park entrance is 21 miles southeast of Paducah, on U.S. Highway 641. Purchase Parkway and Interstate 24 have exits to the park.

Golden Fried Lake Catfish

4 pounds fresh Kentucky Lake catfish fillets
3 cups cornmeal
1 cup plain flour
1 1/2 teaspoons black pepper
3 tablespoons salt
1 tablespoon paprika
1 teaspoon garlic powder

Cut fillets into serving-sized pieces and set aside. Mix the remaining
ingredients together. Wash the fillets and coat with the mixture. For
best results, place breaded fish in refrigerator for awhile before frying.
Fry in deep fat fryer at 350 degrees for 8 to 10 minutes.

Serves 6 to 8

Village Hush Puppies

1 cup self-rising cornmeal
1/2 cup self-rising flour
1 teaspoon salt
1/4 teaspoon garlic powder
2 tablespoons dry chives, chopped
1/4 teaspoon paprika
1/4 cup onions, minced
3/4 cup buttermilk

Mix together all ingredients. Heat oil in deep fryer to 300 degrees. Shape hush puppy mixture with very small ice cream scoop or teaspoon and drop into hot oil. Cook for approximately five minutes or until golden brown.

Makes 12 to 16 hush puppies

The oldest state resort park on the lakes has grown more beautiful and graceful with age. Kenlake State Resort Park, located on the west bank of Kentucky Lake in the southwestern part of the lakes region, embraces each visitor with its easy Southern charm.

As soon as one turns off busy Kentucky Highway 94 onto the stately tree-lined avenue leading up to the main hotel and dining room, relaxation is inescapable. Acres of gently rolling hills, woods, and well-manicured lawns are found along a wide expanse of Kentucky Lake.

There are numerous brightly and comfortably furnished cottages for rent in addition to the 48 rooms at the hotel; all of the latter are graced with either a park or lake view.

Kenlake offers the only tennis center in the state's park system and is open year round. The park boasts four heated and air conditioned indoor courts, plus five outdoor lighted courts. The outdoor courts have windscreens as well as a lakeside 1,200-seat spectator court. Tennis lessons are taught by the center's experienced staff, and tennis wear, shoes, and racquets to rent or buy are found in the pro shop. Special weekend packages are offered throughout the year.

A marina, operated year round, offers boat rentals and full services for fishermen. The broad reaches of water at this

Kenlake State Resort Park

location make sailing ideal. Other recreational facilities include 90 camp sites, a recreation room with video games, bumper pool, and table tennis, a nine-hole golf course, horseback riding, a swimming pool, hiking trails, and four spacious playgrounds for children. A trained recreation leader for adults and children organizes daily activities and special events. A gift shop in the lodge offers a large selection of Kentucky handicraft items.

The magnificent view of the southern portion of Kentucky Lake draws each visitor to the dining room of the hotel, where interest is quickly attracted to the menu and its splendid choices.

Kentucky Country Ham

15-pound country ham
brown sugar
whole cloves

Take a large pot into which the ham to be cooked fits easily after the back end is sawed off. Scrub ham with a brush. Completely cover ham with cold water and soak overnight. Pour off water. Put ham into pot again and cover with hot water. Bring to a boil. After water reaches boiling point, allow to boil 60 minutes. Remove from heat and place pot on padded material. Cover lid tightly with aluminum foil. Wrap pot tightly in newspapers. Cover the entire pot with rugs, blankets and any other material that will keep heat in the pot. Wrapping makes a fireless cooker. Leave pot wrapped tightly overnight. Remove ham the next day and wash it off. Trim excess fat and rind. Score fat side, rub with brown sugar and garnish with whole cloves. Place in a 300-degree oven and bake for one hour.

Proprietor: Commonwealth of Kentucky.

Address: Kenlake State Resort Park, 542 Kenlake Road, Hardin, KY 42048.

Telephone: (502) 474-2211. Toll-free: 1-800-255 PARK or 1-800-325-0143.

Hours: Dining room serves breakfast from 7:00 a.m. to 10:30 a.m.; lunch, 11:30 a.m. to 2:00 p.m.; dinner, 5:00 p.m. to 9:00 p.m. Overnight guests check in after 4:00 p.m.; checkout time is 11:00 a.m. in cottages, noon in lodge.

Season: Open year round.

Seating: Reservations not necessary for dining.

Credit cards: American Express, Visa, MasterCard, and Discover.

Directions: Midway down the western shore of Kentucky Lake, on Kentucky Highway 94 half a mile south of U.S. Highway 68 and Kentucky Highway 80, 15 miles northeast of Murray.

One of the oldest and most unusual state parks in Kentucky is located only eight miles south of Dawson Springs.

Pennyrile Forest State Resort Park had its beginning in the late 1920s when the U. S. Government purchased 14,700 acres in the heart of the West Kentucky coalfields. This land was reforested into a dense and beautiful woodland and, in 1934, the Works Progress Administration developed 300 acres for recreation. In 1956, the entire area, which had expanded to some 18,000 acres, was deeded to the Commonwealth of Kentucky. The 863 acres which now make up the resort itself are nestled deep within what is, perhaps, the most beautiful woods in West Kentucky.

The 24-room Pennyrile Lodge sits high upon the bluff overlooking Lake Beshear and offers a spacious dining room with a wide selection of foods and a spectacular view. Lodging accommodations include 13 cottages of varying sizes and 68 campsites for camping with water and electrical hookups.

The beauty of this rustic wonderland is enhanced even more by tranquil and picturesque Lake Beshear. A sand beach skirts this 55-acre body of water, which also has a convenient bathhouse complex. Guests can take in the spectacular scenery of steep cliffs, deep woods, and calming water by hiking over trails in the forest or making use of the horseback riding facilities in the park. Recreational opportunities

Pennyrile Forest State Resort Park

include fishing in Lake Beshear, boating and golfing, picnicking, shuffleboard, and tennis. In addition to the beach, one can swim in the pool at the lodge. Daily activities and special events for adults and children are under the guidance of a trained recreation director.

For nature lovers, naturalists, or people who simply wish to relax away from the crowds, Pennyrile Forest State Resort Park offers something for everyone. In a state system with many outstanding parks and resorts, Pennyrile has a captivating charm of its own.

Spoon Bread

1 cup white, stone-ground cornmeal
1 1/2 teaspoons salt
2 cups boiling water
4 tablespoons (1/2 stick) margarine, melted
2 tablespoons flour
3 teaspoons baking powder
3 eggs, beaten
1 13-ounce can evaporated milk
bacon grease

Preheat oven to 450 degrees. Pour cornmeal and salt into a mixing bowl. Add water and mix. Pour margarine over the mixture and stir until evenly moistened. In another bowl, mix flour and baking powder with eggs and evaporated milk. Pour eggs and milk mixture into cornmeal mixture and stir until well blended. Grease a 1 1/2- quart baking dish at least 2 1/2 inches deep with bacon grease and pour in batter. Bake until top is lightly browned and tester toothpick comes out clean, or for about 30 minutes.

Serves 6 to 8

Proprietor: Commonwealth of Kentucky.

Address: Pennyrile Forest State Resort Park, 20781 Pennyrile Lodge Road, Dawson Springs, KY 42408-9212.

Telephone (502) 797-3421. Toll-free: 1-800-255-PARK or 1-800-325-1711.

Hours: Dining room serves breakfast from 7:00 a.m. to 10:30 a.m.; lunch, 11:30 a.m. to 2:30 p.m.; dinner, 5:30 p.m. to 9:00 p.m. Overnight guests check in after 4:00 p.m.; checkout time is 11:00 a.m. cottages, noon in lodge.

Season: Open April 1 through October 31.

Seating: Reservations not necessary in dining room.

Credit cards: American Express, Visa MasterCard, and Discover.

Directions: In West Kentucky on Kentucky Highway 109, between Dawson Springs and Hopkinsville.

Legend has it that Ed McMahon mentioned Knoth's Bar-B-Que on the Johnny Carson Show back in 1966, proclaiming it to have the best barbecue he had ever eaten. The very next day there were cars in the parking lot waiting for Knoth's to open, and it has been a popular place ever since.

And the restaurant's popularity with Hollywood continues. In 1995, a coupon for Knoth's appeared in a local paper which mistakenly read "one free glass of ice water with coupon." Jay Leno got a hold of the ad and featured it on his show, and now there is a signed picture of him in the restaurant with his message, "Yo, Knoth's! Thanks for the water!"

Leno mispronounced the name of the restaurant, as do many tourists, but they can tell you Knoth's barbecue is truly some of the best they've ever eaten. Fisherman, tourists, and locals make it a routine to stop by for lunch or dinner in the summer season. Lyon Countians are known to mark their calendars with the dates Hugh Edward Knoth opens in March and closes in November. It's a long dry spell for people who don't remember to stock their freezers with the delicious hickory-smoked barbecue with its unique sweet and sour sauce.

Knoth's is authentic barbecue — visitors to the Lakes Region look for the wood stacked out back and the smoke rising from the pits. For over thirty years, this family-owned business has been cooking pork and beef over wood charcoal

Knoth's Bar-B-Que

the old-fashioned way. Customers reserve shoulders of barbecue for summer picnics and family reunions as well as holidays. Out-of-state visitors have been known to leave Kentucky with Knoth's barbecue and a couple of extra bottles of the famous Knoth's Bar-B-Que Sauce in their suitcases. (Both the hot and mild varieties are also available by mail order.)

A second Knoth's has recently opened in Murray, featuring the same delicious menu as the original. Both establishments cater parties, and both have the secret-recipe barbecue sauce available for sale.

Hugh Edward and his wife Angela run the restaurant operations. Their staff of waitresses is efficient, West-Kentucky friendly, and delight in giving directions or information to people visiting Kentucky and Barkley lakes.

No visit to West Kentucky is complete without a visit to Knoth's Bar-B-Que!

Proprietors: Hugh Edward and Angela Knoth.

Addresses: 7378 U.S. Highway 62 West, Kuttawa, KY 42055. 3975 U.S. Highway 641 North, Murray, KY 42071.

Telephone: Kuttawa: (502) 362-8580. Murray: (502) 759-1712

Hours: Kuttawa: Open Monday through Saturday from 11:00 a.m. to 8:00 p.m. Closed Sunday. Murray: Open Tuesday through Saturday from 11:00 a.m. to 9:00 p.m., Sunday from 11:00 a.m. to 3:00 p.m. Closed Monday.

Season: Kuttawa: Open March through mid-November. Murray: Open year round.

Seating: No reservations necessary.

Credit cards: Visa and MasterCard accepted at the Murray restaurant only.

Directions: Kuttawa: Entrance of Barkley Dam off U.S. Highway 62. Murray: 3 miles north of Murray State University on U.S. Highway 641.

Knoth's Bar-B-Que Menu

Pork Plate

Pork Sandwich

Beef Plate

Beef Sandwich

Hamburger

Cheeseburger

Hot Dogs

Grilled Cheese

Pork by the Pound

Beef by the Pound

Whole Shoulders

Off-Premise Catering

One of the more unusual places to eat in West Kentucky is the Kuttawa Harbor Marina, where outside dining is enjoyed while sitting atop a floating dock, gently rocked by the wake from boats passing along the northern shore of Lake Barkley. The scenery is a fascinating tableau of boat owners and fishermen preparing their boats, pilots motoring into or out of the harbor, and sightings of the seaplane as it takes off from or lands on the water. All this while enjoying a Rudyburger, one of the best hamburgers in West Kentucky!

The Rudyburger, named for a previous owner of the marina, is an area legend. Named a "Best Burger" by the *Paducah Sun* and one of the "Great Burgers of Western Kentucky" by *Southern Living* magazine, the Rudyburger is a hefty 1/2 pound creation served on a toasted bun with pickle, lettuce, tomato, and sautéed onions. Some say the secret to the Rudyburger's taste is in the secret spices used in the sautéed onions; others say it is in the quality of the sirloin steak used to make the burger.

The fries served at the Kuttawa Harbor Marina make an excellent accompaniment to the Rudyburger, as do the old-fashioned milk shakes, made with whole milk and three large scoops of premium ice cream. For the truly adventurous, the Rudy Royale is a meal all by itself, featuring five large scoops of ice cream, double servings of chocolate, and caramel syrup, all topped with whipped cream, strawberry preserves, crushed nuts, and a cherry. It takes two or more people to even make a dent in this gigantic dessert.

Kuttawa Harbor Marina

The atmosphere at the Kuttawa Harbor Marina is casual — diners place their orders at the counter and then the food is delivered to them when ready. For those who prefer to dine indoors, the restaurant features tables at big picture windows from which to watch the harbor activities. Many start the day off with a dockside breakfast, choosing from omelettes, eggs prepared to order, breakfast sandwiches, or lighter fare such as cereal or muffins.

The marina features a number of water-related activities. Browse the marina's nautical gift shop for antique model ships, nautical wear, fishing supplies, and boating accessories. Rent wave runners, fishing boats, pontoons, and ski boats and enjoy the day on the lake. The truly adventurous can sign up for a seaplane ride. Enjoy the nearby picnic area, beach, and park, or just throw a line in by the side of the lake and join the other anglers waiting for the "big one" to strike!

Kuttawa Harbor Marina

Proprietors: Bob and Linda Huebschman.

Address: 1709 Lake Barkley Drive, Kuttawa, KY 42055.

Telephone: (502) 388-9563.

Hours: March 1st until Memorial Day weekend, open 7 days a week from 7:00 a.m. until dusk. Memorial Day weekend until Labor Day weekend, open 7:00 a.m. to 8:00 p.m. Sunday through Thursday; Friday and Saturday open 7:00 a.m. to 9:00 p.m. Labor Day until the weekend before Thanksgiving, open 7 days a week from 7:00 a.m. until dusk.

Season: Closed from December through February.

Seating: No reservations necessary.

Credit cards: All major credit cards.

Directions: From Interstate 24, exit 40: approximately 1.5 miles east on U.S. Highway 62. Turn right onto Kentucky Highway 295; stay on it for two miles to the marina. From West Kentucky Factory Outlet Mall: approximately 3/4 miles west on U.S. Highway 62. Turn left onto Kentucky Highway 295 South, stay on 295 South about 1.5 miles to the marina.

Crabmeat Cracker Spread

First layer:
2 tablespoons Worcestershire sauce
12 ounces cream cheese, softened
1 tablespoon lemon juice
2 tablespoons mayonnaise
1 tablespoon dry minced onion
dash of garlic salt

Second layer:
1/2 bottle (6 ounces) chili sauce

Third layer:
6 1/2 ounces canned crabmeat, drained
chopped parsley

Mix all ingredients for the first layer together, and spread into a 9-inch pie plate. Spread chili sauce on top of first layer. Crumble the crabmeat and sprinkle it over the chili sauce. Sprinkle parsley flakes on top.

Cover and chill for a few hours or overnight. Serve with crackers. (Triscuits are especially good with this!)

Serves 12

Super Dip

1   10-ounce package frozen chopped spinach or broccoli
1 small chopped onion
1 cup sour cream
1 cup mayonnaise
1 can water chestnuts
1 package Knorr dry vegetable soup mix

Cook spinach or broccoli according to package directions. Drain well and cool. Mix with all remaining ingredients and serve with crackers or raw vegetables.

Serves 12

This dip makes a sensational party centerpiece when served in a hollowed-out loaf of sourdough bread surrounded by beautifully cut fresh vegetables. Guests will rave!

Cucumber Sandwiches

1 loaf party rye bread
2 cucumbers, peeled and thinly sliced
1 jar Miracle Whip
garlic powder
seasoned salt

Place party rye bread slices on a flat serving tray. Spread Miracle Whip on each slice of bread. Place a slice of cucumber on each slice of bread. Sprinkle garlic powder and then seasoned salt onto each slice of bread and cucumber.

Serves 15

Try this recipe for an easy-to-prepare yet elegant party appetizer!

The phenomenon of low-fat cooking has reached West Kentucky in the form of the Lite Site Bakery & Cafe. This delightful eatery specializes in low-fat, fat-free and sugar-free baked goods. A breakdown of calories and fat grams is listed on the menu for each dish served at the Lite Side, although one would never guess the hearty and tasty food is actually "lite"!

Delicious aromas from the bakery waft over the diners as they sit in the airy cafe. Big picture windows with flowered chintz curtains let in light from the outside, and the comfortable patio furniture contributes to the illusion of garden dining. Colorful quilts hang from the walls, and there is a small gift shop selling everything from rocks painted with seaside tableaux to low-fat cookbooks.

All the food served at the Lite Side is made from scratch, to ensure the quality and the healthy contents of each dish. For breakfast try a Mesa Waffle, a wonderful, fiber-packed treat made from sweet potatoes. The Mandarin Orange Waffle is made with non-fat yogurt and cholesterol-free eggs, and the Silver Dollar Pancakes have only 150 calories!

Lunches at the Lite Side are an adventure in good eating. Homemade soups and sandwiches are on the menu daily, as are the famous Chicken Enchiladas. The Spicy Black Bean Burger is frequently requested by dedicated locals, and a steamed veggie plate and fresh fruit plate are available as well.

Lite Side Bakery & Cafe

Lite Side owner and chef Irene Bryan has developed a number of innovative dishes for supper. Low-fat, exotic meats like bison and ostrich often appear on the menu, and Friday and Saturday night dinners always feature at least one bison dish, such as bison burgers, bison pot roast, bison barbecue, or bison ribs. Seafood is either boiled or steamed, and ostrich is served in sandwiches, roasts, stir-fry, and as "osh-kabobs"!

The low-fat, non-fat, and sugar-free muffins are best-sellers at the Lite Side Bakery. Black Forest, Burst of Apple, Carrot Raisin, Chocolate, Pumpkin, Raspberry Lemon, and Almond Poppy Seed are a few examples of the large, ever-changing variety of these fabulous treats. Also offered are apple dumplings, sugar-free turnovers, fat-free brownies, and low-fat cream puffs. Loaves of sourdough and French bread sell quickly, and the hamburger buns are always gone before noon! The Lite Side ships muffins and bread anywhere, but a call-ahead order is necessary to make sure there is enough to fill the order.

Come to the Lite Side Bakery & Cafe and experience the cutting edge of healthy and delicious cuisine!

Proprietor: Irene Bryan.

Address: 106 Lake Barkley Drive, Grand Rivers, KY 42045.

Telephone: (502) 362-4586.

Hours: Breakfast, 7:00 a.m. to 11:00 a.m., lunch 11:00 a.m. to 3:00 p.m., dinner, 5:00 p.m. to 9:00 p.m. Open Wednesday through Sunday.

Season: Open year round.

Seating: No reservations necessary.

Credit cards: Not accepted.

Directions: Take exit 31 off Interstate 24 to Grand Rivers. Located in downtown Grand Rivers in the Ridgetop Mall.

Sugar–Free Orange Poppy Seed Muffins

8 egg whites
1/2 cup canola oil
1 1/4 cup unsweetened apple juice concentrate
3/4 cup plus 1 tablespoon orange juice concentrate
1 tablespoon poppy seeds
1 1/2 teaspoons cinnamon
2 3/4 cups flour
2 1/2 teaspoons baking soda

Fill large muffin pans with muffin pan liners. In large mixer combine egg whites, canola oil, juices, and poppy seeds. Beat 1 minute. Add dry ingredients except soda and beat 2 minutes. Stir in soda quickly by hand, about 20 or 30 stirs. Immediately pour into muffin cups. Bake at 325 degrees for 15 minutes, then lower temperature to 300 degrees for 5 minutes.

Makes 1 dozen

Each muffin contains:
fat: 5.6 g
calories: 199

This fabulous sugar-free recipe can also be baked into a cake!

Poppy Seed
Fat-Free Salad Dressing

1/3 white onion, grated
1 cup sugar
6 packets Sweet 'N Low
2 teaspoons dry mustard
2/3 cup white vinegar
2 cups liquid butter buds
2 tablespoons poppy seeds

Place all ingredients into blender and blend until smooth.

Makes 20 2-tablespoon servings

Each serving contains:
fat: 0.5 g
cholesterol: 0 mg
fiber: 0 g
protein: 0 g
carbohydrate: 18 g
sodium: 176 mg
calories: 56

Breakfast Quesadilla

2 flour tortillas
98% fat-free cheddar cheese spread
1/4 cup scrambled egg substitute
1/4 cup chopped Canadian bacon
1 tablespoon chives
salsa and fat-free sour cream for garnish

Heat grill to 350 degrees; coat with non-stick cooking spray. Spread cheese spread onto 1 side of each tortilla. Spread the scrambled egg substitute and Canadian bacon evenly over the cheese-covered side of one tortilla. Then sprinkle the chives evenly over these ingredients. Place on grill. Lay the second tortilla on top, cheese side down. Spray non-stick cooking spray on side facing up. Grill until bottom becomes slightly browned, flip and grill opposite side. For a crunchier tortilla, grill longer. Garnish with salsa and fat-free sour cream.

Serves 1

Each serving contains:
fat: 8 g
calories: 375

Pasta Primavera

1 cup chopped yellow onion
1 cup diced carrots
1 cup broccoli flowerets
1 tablespoon olive oil
1 cup sliced mushrooms
1/2 cup chopped zucchini
1 28-ounce can crushed tomatoes, drained
1 clove garlic, minced
1 tablespoon dried leaf basil
1/4 teaspoon salt
1/4 teaspoon ground black pepper
1/4 teaspoon nutmeg
1 cup frozen green peas, thawed
3 cups cooked fettuccine
1/3 cup grated Parmesan cheese

Assemble all ingredients and utensils in order to prepare ingredients quickly. Sauté the onion, carrots, and broccoli in oil. When the onion begins to soften add the mushrooms and zucchini and sauté 5 more minutes. Add the tomatoes, garlic, basil, salt, pepper, and nutmeg. Simmer for 5 minutes. Add the peas and heat through. Toss with cooked fettuccine and sprinkle Parmesan cheese over all.

Makes 6 1-cup servings

Each serving contains:
fat: 5 g
calories: 214
cholesterol: 4 mg
fiber: 3 g
sodium: 436 mg
carbohydrates: 36 g

Veggie Quiche

1 cup low-fat milk
3/4 cup egg substitute
2 cups broccoli
2 cups asparagus
2 cups cauliflower
2 cups green beans
1/4 cup dried green peppers*
1/2 cup shredded low-fat mozzarella cheese
1 1/2 teaspoon dill
2 tablespoons grated Parmesan cheese

In a large bowl, mix milk and egg substitute. Stir in vegetables, peppers, low-fat cheese, onions, and dill. Spray a 9-inch pie plate with non-stick cooking spray. Pour mixture into pan and sprinkle with Parmesan cheese. Bake at 375 degrees for 30 minutes or until cheese is not runny.

Serves 4

Each serving contains:
fat: 3 g
calories: 136
cholesterol: 19 mg
cholesterol: 0 mg if made without cheese

*Freeze-dried green peppers can be found in the spice section of most groceries.

Miss Scarlett's provides their guests with freshly prepared quality food served in a relaxed Southern atmosphere.

Located on top of a hill in a freeway-close location convenient for travelers, it is open for breakfast, lunch, and dinner. Owner Carl Hamilton takes pride in using only the freshest natural ingredients — farm-fresh eggs, butter, and cream. The steaks are cut daily on the premises from USDA choice, corn-fed beef aged to perfection. Homemade yeast rolls are made fresh everyday, as are the homemade soups and chili.

Start the morning with country ham, blueberry pancakes, Belgian waffles, Eggs Benedict, potato cakes, or sausage-sawmill gravy and biscuits. Accompanied by a hot cup of coffee, the hearty breakfasts fortify both travelers and locals for a long day of sightseeing or outdoor recreation or another day at the office! Opening bright and early at 6:00 a.m., Miss Scarlett's is ready when you are to assist in jump-starting the day.

Lunch patrons can choose light or hearty meals. A wide variety of sandwiches is offered. The famous Scarlett's Hot Brown, a popular variation on the traditional Kentucky Hot Brown, turkey club, grilled chicken breast, Philly-steak, or open-faced roast beef will satisfy the hungriest appetite. Choose a bowl of soup or chili, or one of the artfully designed salads such as taco, chef's, or the Miss Scarlett's specialty, grilled chicken salad. The ever-popular dinner salad & loaded baked potato combo is sure to satisfy!

Miss Scarlett's Restaurant

Start dinner off with a choice of appetizers. The bloomin' onion is a much-loved favorite, as are the hot wings, mozzarella sticks, fried vegetables, and mushroom caps. Try the specialty dinner, a one-pound pork chop, center-cut, marinated, and charbroiled to perfection. Choose from a number of different cut steaks — filet mignon, New York strip, T-bone, sirloin, or ribeye - - all cut from tender, choice, well-aged beef and grilled to order. For traditional Southern fare, order farm-raised or Cajun blackened catfish, country ham, chicken and dumplings, or jumbo fried shrimp. All dinners are served with baked potato or seasoned steak fries, a salad and homemade rolls.

Bright, open, and cheerful, Miss Scarlett's is a great place to bring the children. They will enjoy ordering from their own special menu, and will have a hard time deciding between chicken tenders, hot dog, kid's hamburger, or grilled cheese sandwich. Step into Miss Scarlett's and enjoy the fine food, relaxing atmosphere, and Southern hospitality!

Proprietors: Carl Hamilton and Teddy Wynn.

Address: 708 Complex Drive, Grand Rivers, KY 42045.

Telephone: (502) 928-3126.

Hours: Breakfast is served from 6:00 a.m. to 11:00 a.m.; lunch from 11:00 a.m. to 4:00 p.m.; dinner from 4:00 p.m. to 9:00 p.m. Open Friday and Saturday until 10:00 p.m.

Season: Open year round; closed Thanksgiving and Christmas Day.

Seating: Reservations are recommended.

Credit cards: American Express, Visa, MasterCard, and Discover.

Directions: Located off exit 31 of Interstate 24 next to the Best Western Hotel, 2 miles north of Kentucky Dam.

Eggs Benedict

8 large eggs
8 slices smoked Canadian bacon
4 sourdough English muffins, split in halves

Hollandaise sauce:
6 egg yolks
3/4 teaspoon salt
3/4 teaspoon Tabasco sauce
1/2 tablespoon lemon juice
1/2 cup butter

Using a traditional egg poacher, steam poach eggs approximately 3 minutes. At the same time, grill the Canadian bacon and toast the English muffins. Place 1 slice of bacon on top of toasted English muffin half and top with a poached egg. Make 8 of these sandwiches and keep hot.

To make sauce: Melt butter and set aside. Beat egg yolks until uniform yellow color. Add salt, Tabasco sauce, and lemon juice and mix well. Pour butter into mixture in a thin stream while beating with a wire wisk.

Serve 2 sandwiches on a plate with a ramekin of Hollandaise sauce on the side.

Serves 4

The trick to this dish is getting everything to come out at the same time! Miss Scarlett's serves the Hollandaise sauce on the side in individual ramekins rather than ladled over the top of each egg. Delicious either way!

Mushroom Strata

1 pound sliced mushrooms
4 tablespoons butter
1/2 cup chopped green onions
1/2 cup chopped celery
1/2 cup chopped green pepper
3/4 teaspoon salt
1/4 teaspoon pepper
2 tablespoons parsley
1/2 cup mayonnaise
6 slices firm white bread
1/4 cup grated Parmesan or Romano cheese
2 cups milk
3 eggs

Sauté mushrooms in butter for a few minutes until slightly limp. Add onions, celery, green pepper, salt, pepper, and parsley and cook about 3 minutes longer. Remove from heat, stir in mayonnaise, and set aside. Remove crusts from bread and cut into 1-inch squares. Put half the bread in a greased 2 1/2 quart casserole. Spoon mushroom mixture over bread in casserole, then cover with the remaining bread. Beat eggs and milk together until frothy; pour over casserole. Refrigerate, covered, 1 hour or overnight. Bake, uncovered, at 325 degrees for 50 minutes. Sprinkle cheese on top and bake an additional 10 minutes until golden brown.

Serves 6

Country French Bread

4 cups flour
1 tablespoon sugar
1 teaspoon salt
1 package dry yeast (not quick-rising)
1 cup lukewarm water

Combine yeast and water in a bowl. In another bowl, sift flour, sugar, and salt together. Add dry ingredients to the yeast. Stir together, adding more lukewarm water if needed until mixture sticks together and is moist. Cover bowl with a clean towel and put it out to rise in a warm (about room temperature on a summer's day) place. During the rising, punch down the dough at least twice. (Punch down dough by placing a fist into the dough and pushing down to the bottom of the bowl to make a deep crater, then flip the dough over and re-cover the bowl with the towel.) Let rise for 2 to 4 hours. Divide dough in half and place into 2 oven-proof bowls that have been greased and floured. Cover with towels and let rise for 1 more hour. Bake in the bowls at 400 degrees for about 1 hour, until toothpick comes out clean.

Makes 2 loaves

Scarlett's Hot Brown

2 homemade large dinner rolls
2 ounces shaved smoked turkey
2 ounces shaved smoked ham
1 cup Trio Cheeze Sauce
1/2 ounce canned pimientos
1 ounce real bacon crumbles
4 slices ripe tomatoes
1 ounce shredded cheddar cheese
fresh chives, chopped
fresh parsley sprigs
1/2 cherry tomato

Slice dinner rolls and place on a plate. Shred shaved smoked turkey and ham on top of sliced rolls. Mix cheese sauce and pimientos. Pour cheese sauce mix on top of turkey and ham. Sprinkle bacon crumbles on top, and place sliced tomatoes on top of this. Distribute shredded cheddar over sandwich and top with chives. Bake at 350 degrees for 5 to 7 minutes. Remove from oven. Garnish with fresh parsley and 1/2 cherry tomato.

Serves 1

Kentucky Oysters

1 medium eggplant
1 small onion
4 cups Ritz cracker crumbs
1 cup milk
2 tablespoons butter

Peel eggplant and cut in half lengthwise. Scoop out most of the seeds and cut the remaining pulp into 1/2-inch squares. Dice the onion and boil, along with the eggplant, in salted water until both are limp. Drain well, and layer in buttered casserole dish. Spread cracker crumbs on top and dot with butter. Bake at 350 degrees for 35 minutes.

Serves 6

It is truly amazing how much this vegetable dish tastes like oysters! *A* wonderful accompaniment to grilled meats.

Colonel Bill Newsom and his daughter Nancy Mahaffey own and manage a small country store with an international reputation. Housed in a mill built in 1850, Newsom's Old Mill Store sells everything you would expect to see in a country store — seed, plants, country condiments, pottery, sorghum, memorabilia, rag rugs, candy by the barrel, and sandwiches to order.

The main draw to Newsom's, though, is Colonel Bill's aged Kentucky country hams. The Newsom family has been dry-curing hams in Kentucky and Virginia ever since they first arrived from England in the mid-1600s. The family has lived in the Princeton, Kentucky, area since 1798, and Colonel Bill and Nancy carry on the tradition of making some of the best country hams in the world.

The ham has been praised to the skies by over one hundred food editors, including those from *Food and Wine*, *Connoisseur*, *Bon Appetit*, and *True Grits*. The hams are so fabulous that Julia Child and James Beard have used them in their cooking.

The process that Newsom's hams go through before they are put up for sale is long and involved, and is done to ensure the fabulous taste and high quality of each ham. The Newsoms take pride in the fact that they do not use sodium nitrite or nitrates to cure their hams, as most country-ham producers do.

Newsom's Old Mill Store

All their hams are hand rubbed with a special salt and sugar cure. The hams are resalted several days later, then housed for a month or two in a special room to ensure the proper temperature during salt penetration. They are then moved to the smokehouse, where they are hung up and smoked over a fire of green hickory wood and sawdust that burns slowly in an old iron wash kettle.

After the smoking is complete, the hams are left hanging through Kentucky's changing temperatures as the hams undergo the "July Sweat," which gives them their distinctive flavor. Finished hams weigh between 13 and 17 pounds, though larger ones are sometimes available.

During the summer, Newsom's is filled with fresh,

locally grown produce that will make your mouth water. Pick up a country ham while you are there. If you're not in the neighborhood, pick up the phone and order one to be shipped to you. Bacon, sausage, smoked barbecue ham, and country jams, jellies, and relishes are also available by mail (catalogs are mailed upon request). Mail order service is personalized and quick.

Newsom's is a great place to find that unique Kentucky item that will be enjoyed by the folks back home!

Proprietors: Colonel Bill Newson and his daughter Nancy Mahaffey.

Address: 208 East Main Street, Princeton, KY 42445.

Telephone: (502) 365-2482. (This is the number for the Old Mill Store and the mail-order service.)

Hours: Monday through Saturday from 8:30 a.m. to 5:00 p.m.

Season: Open all year.

Credit cards: Visa and MasterCard.

Directions: From Interstate 24: take exit 56, turn right off exit onto route 139. Go 10 miles into Princeton, turn right at first stop light, then turn right at second stop sign onto East Main. The Old Mill Store is located at the end of the historic business district on the right. From Western Kentucky Parkway: take exit 13 to Princeton. Turn left off exit onto Highway 293 North. Go 1 to 2 miles to courthouse. Turn left onto Main Street. Go one block; Newsom's is on the right.

Boiled Kentucky Country Ham

1 Kentucky country ham
1 cup brown sugar or molasses
1/2 cup cider vinegar
black pepper or ham glaze of choice
   (see recipes on following page)

Soak ham overnight in cold water. If the ham has been aged over 15 months, soak two nights in cold water, changing the water after each night.

Clean ham with warm water and a bristle brush. Place cleaned ham in large container and completely cover with water. Add brown sugar or molasses and vinegar. Bring to a boil and reduce heat. Simmer (do not boil) about 20 minutes per pound or until meat thermometer registers 170 degrees. Ham is done when bone in hock just begins to shake loose easily.

Turn off heat and allow ham to cool in the broth, returning moisture to the ham. Remove ham from broth, skin, and coat with ham glaze or cover with black pepper. Bake at 400 degrees long enough for it to get golden brown and glazed.

Country Ham Glaze

Any of the following glazes are fabulous on Newsom's Kentucky Country Ham:

* Mix brown sugar with enough cider vinegar, fruit juice, cider or juice from pickled peaches to make a paste. Coat ham.

* Coat ham with mixture of 1 cup brown sugar and 2 tablespoons flour or 1/4 cup fine bread crumbs.

* Coat ham with mixture of 1 cup brown sugar and 1 cup drained, crushed pineapple.

* Spread ham with a very thin layer of prepared mustard, then coat ham liberally with brown sugar.

* Coat ham with mixture made of 1 pound brown sugar, 1 or 2 tablespoons dry mustard, and enough sherry to moisten.

Other ideas:

* Baste ham while it is baking with pineapple, cherry, or other fruit juices or with thick brown sugar syrup.

* Decorate top of ham with slices of canned pineapple or other colorful fruits.

To glaze the ham:

Remove skin and, if desired, score fat in 1- or 2-inch squares. Coat with one of the glazes given above or your favorite glaze. Place whole cloves into each square if desired. Bake at 400 degrees until glaze is golden brown and set.

Bite–Size Kentucky Country Ham Hors d'Oeuvres

Filling:
1/2 to 1 pound ground, cooked country ham
1/2 cup or more pickle relish
3 boiled eggs, finely diced
Miracle Whip or Hellmann's mayonnaise, enough to mix
smoothly
sugar to taste (optional)

Mix above ingredients together well.

Bread shells:
About 15 slices white bread (Each slice of bread makes 4
mini-muffin tin shells or 1 shell in a regular size muffin tin.)
1 stick margarine, melted

*Remove crust from bread slices. Mash bread slices and cut four ways.
Dip slices in melted margarine. Press into mini-muffin tins. Bake at
400 degrees until light brown. Remove from oven and cool. Remove
from tins. Spoon small amount of ham salad into baked shells.*

Makes about 5 dozen mini-sized hors d'oeuvres

The Tullar family is proud to welcome you to their award-winning restaurant. Owners Chip and Michael Tullar, their families, and their parents, founders Patti and Bill, make guests feel welcome in their old-time establishment, decorated with barn wood, brick floors, stained glass windows, antiques, and lots of fresh flowers from the extensive Tullar gardens.

Among the many acknowledgments Patti's has garnered over the years, Chip and Mike were honored to be named "Small Business Persons of the Year for Kentucky" in 1995. The awards presentation was held in the White House, and included a hearty congratulations from President Bill Clinton. In 1996, Patti's won *Southern Living* magazine's first annual "Reader's Choice Award" for favorite small-town restaurant in the United States.

Fans of Patti's can easily understand the national acclaim given to the business. Starting out as Hamburger Patti's Ice Cream Parlor in 1977, the popular cafe expanded and changed over the years into the charming 1880s village that it is today, including two restaurants seating 400 people, gift shops, a small zoo for homeless critters, a game room, and an ESPN-qualifying miniature golf course.

Diners are greeted with a smile and Patti's famous flowerpot bread — homemade and warm from the oven, served in individual clay flowerpots accompanied by creamy strawberry butter. Knowledgeable patrons are careful not to fill up before the specialty of the

Patti's 1880s Settlement

house arrives: charbroiled pork chops, seasoned with Patti's secret flavorings, cut two inches thick and weighing close to a pound. During lunch, sample the Tullar's homemade potato chips, delectable sandwiches like Michael's Kentucky Hot Brown, or made-to-order hamburgers with all the trimmings. To add to the unforgettable taste, all sandwiches are served on homemade bread and buns, baked fresh daily. Corn dogs and peanut butter & jelly sandwiches are served all day long for youngsters.

If all the good food, games, and zoo animals aren't enough to keep the children occupied, they can always play with Calvin the lovable swine, Bill's favorite pet. Wearing a specially tailored leash, the jet-black pot-bellied pig follows Bill throughout the gift shops, and is always ready to be petted.

To top off a visit to Patti's, order one of the many luscious desserts on the menu, such as the John Y. Brown Pie, named for the former governor, or Bill's Boat Sinker Pie — a double fudge chocoholic delight! Those with no room to indulge after their meal often stop by the gift shop and pick up one of the pies to take home.

At Patti's, guests may casually stroll around the grounds to see the wishing well waterwheel, antiques, quilts, books, lovely gardens, and gifts acquired from around the world to take home. Bill and Patti often stroll the premises to entertain children with the menagerie of stuffed animals found in Grandmother Tullar's gift shop or to offer directions to the many fine antique and gift shops located in Grand Rivers.

Proprietors: The Tullar family — founders Patti and Bill, owners Chip and Michael, and their families.

Address: Box 111, Grand Rivers, Kentucky 42045.

Telephone: (502) 362-8844.

Hours: Open seven days a week, 10:30 a.m. until 8:30 p.m.

Season: Open year round.

Seating: Reservations suggested. Tour groups welcome.

Credit cards: MasterCard, Visa, and Discover.

Directions: Located 3 miles off exit 31 of Interstate 24 in Grand Rivers. Located 26 miles southeast of Paducah at Kentucky Lake "Twix the Rivers."

Grandmother Tullar's French Dressing

4 teaspoons salt
3 cups vinegar
1 cup water
6 cups sugar
4 cups ketchup
1/2 cup dry mustard
8 tablespoons grated onion
2 3/4 tablespoons paprika
3 cups salad oil

Mix all ingredients except salad oil together. Slowly beat the salad oil into the mixture. Refrigerate.

Derby Day Grits

6 cups water
2 1/2 teaspoons salt
1 1/2 cups quick grits
1/2 cup butter
dash cayenne pepper
2 6-ounce rolls garlic cheese spread
3 eggs, separated
dash paprika

Combine water and salt in 4-quart pan. Bring to a boil. Gradually add grits. Cook over low heat until thickened. Remove from heat. Stir in butter, cheese, and cayenne, stirring until cheese melts. Stir in egg yolks. Beat egg whites until stiff; fold in. Pour into greased casserole dish. Bake at 350 degrees for 45 to 60 minutes or until grits begin to set.

Serves 6

Aunt Mary Ann's Sicilian Meat Roll

2 eggs, beaten
3/4 cup soft bread crumbs (1 slice bread)
1/2 cup tomato juice
2 tablespoons parsley, snipped
1/2 teaspoon oregano
1/4 teaspoon salt
1/4 teaspoon pepper
1 small clove garlic, minced
2 pounds ground beef
8 thin slices boiled ham
6 ounces (1 1/2 cups) shredded mozzarella cheese
3 slices mozzarella cheese (halved diagonally)

Combine first eight ingredients, add meat and mix. Place meat mixture onto a sheet of aluminum foil and pat into a 12 x 10 inch rectangle. Arrange ham slices on top of the meat, leaving margins around the edge. Sprinkle the shredded mozzarella cheese over the ham. Starting from the short end and using the foil to gently lift, carefully roll the meat, jelly roll fashion, into a log. Seal edges and ends. Place the roll seam side down in a 13 x 9 inch baking pan. Bake at 350 degrees for 1 hour and 15 minutes or until done (the roll will be pink). Place the slices of mozzarella cheese on top of the roll and melt for 5 minutes.

Serves 6 to 8

John Y. Brown Pie

1 cup sugar
1/2 cup flour
1/2 cup melted butter
2 eggs, slightly beaten
6 ounces butterscotch chips
1 cup pecan pieces
1 teaspoon vanilla
1 9-inch unbaked pie shell

Mix together sugar and flour. Add the melted butter and blend well. Stir in the eggs, butterscotch chips, pecans, and vanilla. Pour into the pie shell. Bake at 325 degrees for 60 minutes or until golden brown. Pie will wiggle when it is done and then set as it cools.

Serves 8

Coconut Pie with Mile–High Meringue

Pie filling:
3/4 cup sugar
3 tablespoons cornstarch
1/4 teaspoon salt
3 egg yolks, slightly beaten
2 cups milk
2 tablespoons butter
1 teaspoon vanilla
1 cup shredded coconut
1 9-inch baked pie crust

Meringue:
4 egg whites
1/2 teaspoon baking powder
1/2 cup sugar

For the pie filling: Combine dry ingredients and mix well. Add egg yolks and stir. Add milk and cook slowly, stirring constantly until thick. When the pudding is thick, remove from heat and add butter, vanilla, and coconut. Pour the mixture into cooled, baked crust.

For the meringue: Beat egg whites with baking powder until stiff. Add sugar and blend well. Cover pie with mixture, making sure to seal the filling to edge of crust. Brown in 350 degree oven approximately 15 minutes.

Variation: For pineapple pie, substitute 1 cup well-drained crushed pineapple for coconut.

Serves 8

Strawberry Butter

3/4 pound margarine or butter
16 ounces frozen strawberries
1/2 cup powdered sugar

Bring margarine or butter to room temperature and whip. Let strawberries thaw, saving strawberry juice. Whip all ingredients together,
including strawberry juice, with large mixer. Fresh strawberries can
be used in season. Vary amount of sugar to taste, increasing sugar when
using frozen berries and decreasing when using fresh berries.

Drive by The Pelican restaurant anytime during the day or night and there will be cars in the parking lot and people inside enjoying a hearty meal. A favorite dining spot for local West Kentuckians and visiting sportsmen, The Pelican has been in continuous operation since 1956, when it opened as a small snack bar. The restaurant has been expanded over the years to its present 150-person seating capacity. The current owners, Bill and Rody Cullen, have been at the Pelican since 1973.

The Pelican has become a West Kentucky landmark, noted for its delicious home style cooking and wide variety of breakfasts available around the clock. Fishermen and hunters stop by before dawn to order the Sportsman's Special — two eggs, two hotcakes, ham, bacon or sausage, hash browns, and toast or biscuits — a substantial meal that will fortify them for whatever they will face that day in the forest or on the lakes. Workers just coming off the night shift enjoy the Working Man's Special, a robust meal of two eggs, ham, home fries, grits or gravy, and biscuits. Other favorites include steak 'n' egg, country ham, and pork tenderloin breakfasts with all the extras. The homemade biscuits and milk gravy are legendary.

Plate lunches are served daily until 9 p.m. Choose roast beef or roast pork, pulled hickory-smoked barbecue, chicken tenders, or spaghetti and a variety of vegetables such as coleslaw, whipped potatoes, hush puppies, or fresh vegetables in season. Those with lighter

The Pelican

appetites can choose a fruit plate or the diet special, a charbroiled chicken breast with fruit and vegetables. Gigantic club, Philly - style, and other deluxe sandwiches, chili, soups, and salads are on the menu, and a trip to the salad bar can be added for a small additional charge.

The Pelican's specialty dinner is catfish, served as fiddlers or fillets, prepared fried, broiled, or creole style. Both fresh Kentucky Lake catfish and the milder- tasting farm-raised variety are offered. Seafood, charbroiled steaks and chops, pizza, and special children's meals all contribute to the very crowded menu! Try the fresh strawberry pie in season, or a slice of creamy lemon cheesecake for dessert. The fresh-squeezed lemonade is a must in summer!

Those planning a trip into the Kentucky wilderness stop by the Fisherman's Friend, a bait-and-tackle store right next door. Camping and picnic supplies are also available, as are light snacks. The store is open from 6 a.m. until 10 p.m. in the summer, and from 7 a.m. until 4 p.m. in the winter.

Travelers to West Kentucky won't want to miss a visit to The Pelican, to sample the same appetizing and hearty food enjoyed by locals for decades!

Proprietors: Bill and Rody Cullen.

Address: 1006 U.S. Highway 62, Grand Rivers, KY 42045.

Telephone: (502) 362-8610.

Hours: Open seven days a week, 24 hours a day.

Season: Open all year except Thanksgiving, Christmas Eve, and Christmas Day.

Seating: No reservations necessary.

Credit cards: Visa, MasterCard, and Discover.

Directions: Midway between Kentucky and Barkley dams on U.S. Highway 62 in Lake City. One mile south of exit 31 off Interstate 24.

Chicken Gumbo Soup

1- 2 1/2 to 3 pound chicken, cut up
2 No. 2 1/2 cans tomatoes, chopped
2 bay leaves
1/4 teaspoon black pepper
1 tablespoon chicken base or 2 bouillon cubes
1 teaspoon thyme
1 teaspoon Chef Paul's Poultry magic seasoning
dash Tabasco sauce
1 1/2 quarts water
1 large onion, chopped
2 green peppers, chopped
2 celery stalks, chopped
1 tablespoon margarine
1 cup frozen corn
1 cup frozen, cut okra
1/2 cup rice, uncooked

Add chicken, tomatoes, and spices to water in large kettle and start to simmer. Sauté onions, green peppers, and celery in margarine until vegetables are just tender. Add to soup kettle, and cook until chicken is tender. Remove chicken from soup pot, skin and de-bone, and cut up chicken into bite-sized pieces. Add chicken back to soup kettle along with the frozen vegetables and rice. Simmer until frozen vegetables are tender.

Serves 8

The recipe for this hearty soup is frequently requested by diners at The Pelican.

Pelican Chili

5 cups water
2 No. 2 1/2 cans chili beans
2 No. 2 1/2 cans tomato puree
1 No. 2 1/2 can whole tomatoes, chopped
2 1/2 pounds ground beef
1 green pepper, chopped
1 cup chopped onion
1 tablespoon ground cumin
4 tablespoons chili powder
1 tablespoon cocoa
1/2 tablespoon salt
1/2 tablespoon Tabasco sauce

Put water in large pot and add canned foods. Brown ground beef in large skillet, drain, and add to pot. Simmer onions and green peppers in left-over meat juices until soft, drain, and add to pot. Add spices and stir thoroughly. Bring to a boil, reduce heat, and simmer for 1 1/2 hours.

Serves 8

Bill's Coleslaw

1 cup sugar
1 cup oil
1 cup vinegar
1 teaspoon mustard seed
1 teaspoon celery seed
1 teaspoon salt
1/2 red onion, diced
1 green pepper, diced
3 1/2 quarts shredded cabbage

Mix sugar, oil, and vinegar. Bring to a boil and set aside to cool. Mix with other ingredients and store in closed container.

Serves 8

This is just one of the tasty items on the menu that has made The Pelican famous!

Rody's Strawberry Pie

4 ounces cream cheese
2 tablespoons milk
2 tablespoons sugar
1/4 teaspoon almond extract
1/4 cup chopped pecans
3 pints fresh strawberries
strawberry glaze*
graham cracker crust
whipped topping

Cream together the cream cheese, milk, sugar and almond extract. Spread over the bottom of the crust. Sprinkle with chopped pecans. Mix strawberries with enough glaze to hold them together and add to the pie. Refrigerate. Serve with whipped topping.

Serves 8

* Strawberry glaze can be purchased commercially in the produce section of grocery stores. Or use this recipe:

Strawberry Glaze

1/2 pint strawberries
1/2 cup sugar
1 tablespoon cornstarch
1/4 cup water
2 teaspoons butter

Wash strawberries in cold water and hull. Crush in saucepan. Combine sugar and cornstarch, and stir into crushed strawberries. Add water. Over medium heat, stirring constantly, bring to a boil. Mixture will be thickened and translucent. Strain through a fine wire mesh strainer or sieve. Add butter and allow to cool.

Dixie's Buttermilk Raisin Pie

Pie filling:
1/2 cup raisins
1/2 cup water
2 eggs
juice of 1 lemon
2 cups buttermilk
1 cup sugar
1/4 cup flour
1/2 teaspoon salt
1/2 stick margarine
1 baked pie crust

Meringue:
3 egg whites
1/4 teaspoon cream of tartar
6 tablespoons sugar
1/2 teaspoon vanilla

Cover raisins with water and microwave one minute. Set aside to cool. Beat eggs, lemon juice, and buttermilk together. Add sugar, flour, and salt. Microwave 6 to 8 minutes until thick, stirring every 2 or 3 minutes. Drain raisins and add to mixture. Add margarine and mix. Pour into baked pie shell. To make meringue, beat the egg whites with a mixer on high speed until frothy, add the cream of tartar, and whip until stiff but not dry. Gradually beat in the sugar, adding a little at a time. Beat in vanilla. Cover the pie filling with the meringue. Bake at 350 degrees until lightly browned, about 5 minutes.

Serves 8

Sallie's Chess Pie

Pie filling:
2 cups sugar
1/2 cup butter, melted
4 tablespoons flour
6 egg yolks, well beaten
1 cup milk

Meringue:
3 egg whites
1/4 teaspoon cream of tartar
6 tablespoons sugar
1 teaspoon cinnamon

Combine dry ingredients. Add milk, egg yolks, and butter. Bake at 375 degrees until set, approximately 45 minutes. To make meringue, beat the egg whites with a mixer on high speed until frothy, then add cream of tartar and whip until stiff. Gradually add the sugar while continuing to beat the egg whites. Cover the pie filling with the meringue; sprinkle with cinnamon. Bake at 350 degrees for a few minutes until lightly browned.

Serves 8

The Pines has a a two-decade tradition of serving some of the most meticulously prepared gourmet food in Paducah. Owned by the same family since 1977, Betty and Johnny Box and their daughter and son-in-law Judy and Max Bastani, the restaurant is actually two establishments: the prestigious Pines dining room, with its warm ambiance for elegant dining, or Café Maurice, a cheerful bistro offering lighter fare for lunch as well as ethnic selections in the evening.

The first to establish exhibition cooking in Paducah, Chef Max Bastani is at home behind the glass panes, as he maintains operations at the open rotisserie (imported from France), the live charcoal grill, and the sauté station. Each evening, Max features his own special creations.

Steak, cooked over live charcoal, is a specialty here, and can be ordered with a variety of European sauces such as Marchand de Vin, Au Poivre, Caper, and Bernaise. The grilled fish entrées are delicately prepared in wine sauce and olive oil. The Pines is famous for its rotisserie-style chicken, and the shrimp, scallop, and lobster dishes are popular choices with diners. The spectacular 40-item salad bar offers an assortment of garden fresh vegetables, fresh fruits, gourmet salads, relishes, deli meats, smoked oysters, and a variety of fat-free and low cholesterol dressings.

The Pines and Café Maurice

Stepping into Café Maurice is like stepping into a bistro on the Champs Elysées. Hearty homemade soups and specialty sandwiches tempt the palate, and the ribeye is tender and tasty. Evening fare includes various pasta dishes and delectable shrimp simmered in beer, garlic, and Cajun spices. The complementary bread bar is a much-loved delight, and includes French baguettes, ciabatta (Italian bread), and sourdough. Several flavored European butters are offered to complement the breads.

Café Maurice is a favorite meeting place for coffee and dessert, and offers a variety of coffees from Ireland, France, Spain and Italy as well as the favorites, espresso, cappuccino, and cafe au lait. The desserts are legendary, and present a difficult choice. White Eclair Cake, Turtle Pie, Jack Daniels Chocolate

Ice Cream, and Heavenly Seven Cake are just some of the delectable options.

The restaurant stocks a wide variety of imported and domestic wines available by the glass, as well as a selection of premium liquors and liqueurs.

The Pines banquet room is available for civic clubs, business meetings, and luncheons and will seat 90 comfortably. A children's menu is available.

Proprietors: Max and Judy Bastani.

Address: 900 North 32nd St., Paducah, KY 42001.

Telephone: (502) 442-9304.

Hours: The Pines: Lunch, 11:30 a.m. to 2:00 p.m. Monday through Friday; dinner, 5:00 p.m. to 10:00 p.m. Monday through Saturday. Café Maurice: Open 11:30 a.m. to 10:00 p.m. Monday through Saturday.

Season: Open year round.

Seating: Reservations requested at The Pines, not necessary at Café Maurice.

Credit cards: MasterCard, Visa, American Express, Diner's Club, Carte Blanche, and Discover.

Directions: Take exit 4 off Interstate 24 at Kentucky Oaks Mall and follow the "loop" to 32nd St. Turn right and look for signs on the left.

Mediterranean Bread Spread

1 pound unsalted butter
1/2 cup brine-cured olives (Calamata)
1/3 cup Parmesan cheese
2 whole garlic bulbs
salt and pepper to taste
1 tablespoon fresh thyme
2 tablespoons fresh oregano
1/3 cup virgin olive oil
3 tablespoons brine from olives

Have the butter at room temperature. Pit and chop the Calamata olives. Brush 2 whole garlic bulbs with olive oil and roast at 250 degrees for 20 minutes. Let cool, peel, and puree. Use 1 ounce of the roasted garlic puree in this recipe and reserve the remaining for later use (great in salad dressings, on pasta, or rubbed on grilled meats). Use the paddle attachment on mixer, and mix chopped olives, 1 ounce garlic puree, and all remaining ingredients on medium speed for 3 minutes until creamy. Put in individual ramekins and chill slightly. Serve as a spread on crusty bread.

Makes 1 pound

Ginger Marinade

1 cup soy sauce
1 cup water
1/4 cup dry sherry
1 tablespoon freshly grated ginger
1 tablespoon fresh garlic
1/4 cup shredded carrots
2 green onions, chopped
2 tablespoons diced bell pepper
2 tablespoons diced red bell pepper
1 fresh jalapeno pepper, seeded
zest of one lemon
juice of one lemon
1/4 cup olive oil
olive oil for grilling

Put all ingredients except water, soy sauce, and olive oil for grilling in food processor with chopping blade and chop until coarse in texture. Add water and soy sauce. Marinate fish for 20 minutes, then grill while basting with olive oil until fish is done. Top fish with a tablespoon of marinade and serve.

Use this marinade with any firm-textured white fish. The marinade will keep in the refrigerator for 2 to 3 weeks.

Lentil Soup

1 cup bacon fat
2 cups celery, diced
2 cups onion, diced
2 cups carrots, diced
2 garlic cloves, minced
3 quarts beef stock
1 quart tomato juice
3 bay leaves
1/2 teaspoon black pepper
12 ounces lentils, soaked and drained
1/2 pound smoked sausage
salt, cornstarch, and water as needed
1 fresh tomato, chopped

Sauté celery, onion, carrots, and garlic in bacon fat. Stir in beef stock, tomato juice, bay leaves, and pepper, and bring to a boil. Add lentils and cook on low heat until soft. Add sausage and salt to taste. Cook 10 minutes. Adjust thickness, again add salt to taste, and add chopped tomato.

Makes 5 quarts

Entrecote au Poivre

2 sirloin strip steaks
1 tablespoon green peppercorns
1 tablespoon butter
1 teaspoon green onion, chopped
1 ounce brandy
2/3 cup brown sauce*
1/2 teaspoon fresh parsley, chopped
4 tablespoons heavy cream
salt and pepper as needed

Season steaks; grill to desired doneness and keep warm. Sauté green onion in butter and peppercorns. Saute a minute longer; add brandy. Wait until the flame goes down, then add brown sauce and cream. Season with salt and pepper to taste. Reduce until the sauce is thick enough to coat a spoon. Add parsley, cover steaks, and serve.

Serves 2

*Use your favorite recipe for brown sauce, or try this: Melt 1 1/2 tablespoons butter, then add 1 1/2 tablespoons flour and stir until blended. Stir in 3/4 cup canned bouillon or beef stock. Bring to a boil, stirring constantly.

Parfait au Grand Marnier

2 egg yolks
1/4 cup sugar
4 tablespoons Grand Marnier (reserve 1 tablespoon for garnish)
1/2 pint whipping cream, whipped
2 egg whites, beaten
nutmeg
2 tablespoons whipped cream for garnish

Beat egg yolks and sugar together until lemon-colored. Mix in Grand Marnier. Fold in whipped cream and egg whites. Pour into individual serving glasses and freeze until firm. Garnish with whipping cream, 1 tablespoon Grand Marnier, and nutmeg.

Serves 4

142

Whaler's Catch Restaurant has a rich and varied past. Commonly known as "Whalers" by Paducahans, the first-of-its-kind fresh seafood restaurant and fish market was started in 1977 by Roberta Shelby Morse. In 1990 the restaurant was purchased by John Harris, who has carried on Roberta's tradition of offering daily fresh seafood selections. In early 1996 the 59-year-old building that housed Whaler's Catch burned, causing major structural damage. As a result, John Harris moved the restaurant to its present location in the Johnson building in historic downtown Paducah.

Situated near the banks of the Ohio River, the Johnson Building has been there since before the turn of the century. It has been home to a number of varied enterprises, at one time housing Loeb, Bloom and Company, distillers and dealers of fine Kentucky bourbon. Through the years the building has also been home to a clothing company, an auto top company, a real estate company, and Shoe Workers Local 38.

Though more than a century has passed, the three-story Johnson Building retains a notable amount of ornamental work from days gone by. Adding to the enchanting atmosphere and historical value of the restaurant, visitors to Whaler's Catch will see another grand antique: a hand-carved bar. Built in 1863, the elaborate solid mahogany bar has quite a history. At one point it was located in a tavern in Cairo, Illinois, where General Ulysses S. Grant reportedly bellied up to it during the Civil War.

Whaler's Catch Restaurant & Oyster Bar

Whaler's Catch is packed every night with patrons who return again and again for the delicious fresh seafood dishes, Creole specialties and relaxing atmosphere. It is a gathering place for lovers of raw oysters and shrimp prepared in a variety of ways. The Southern-style gumbo and red beans and rice are prepared in the finest New Orleans tradition.

Plump frog legs, charcoal grilled or batter dipped and fried, are a specialty, along with orange roughy broiled in butter. Whaler's Catch Seafood Salad is famous throughout West

Kentucky and is available at lunch and dinner. Charcoal grilled chicken and steaks are also featured, plus a host of appetizers.

The members of the "Catch Crew" invite you to enjoy the beautifully restored, historic setting, the casual, New Orleans ambiance, and the fine dining that await all who come to Whaler's Catch Restaurant.

Proprietor: John Harris.

Address: 123 N. 2nd St., Paducah, KY 42001.

Telephone: (502) 444-7701.

Hours: Open Monday through Saturday at 11:00 a.m. for lunch. The oyster bar opens at 3:30, and dinner is served from 5:00 p.m. The seafood market is open from 10:00 a.m. to 5:30 p.m.

Season: Open year round.

Seating: Reservations necessary.

Credit cards: Visa, MasterCard, and American Express.

Directions: From Kentucky Dam: Take Interstate 24 exit 16 (9 miles); turn right at the stop sign to Paducah to Junction 62 West (1/4 mile); take a left (5 miles); take a right on West Business 60 (Downtown Loop) to Monroe Street (3 miles). Turn right on Monroe, go 1 block to 2nd Street; take a right. Whaler's is 1 block on the right. From Kentucky Oaks Mall: (Located at exit 4 off Interstate 24); take East Highway 60 (Highway 60 turns into East Business 60); turn left on Monroe, go 2 blocks, and take a right on 2nd Street. Whalers is 1 block on your right. (Travel time from Kentucky Oaks Mall to Whaler's Catch is about 6 minutes.)

Maryland-Style Crab Cakes

2 1/2 pounds blue crab claw meat (picked well)
4 large eggs
2/3 cup Italian bread crumbs
1 tablespoon mustard
1 1/2 teaspoons white pepper
1 tablespoon Tabasco sauce
1 1/2 cups Hellmann's mayonnaise
1/2 cup shredded cheddar cheese
1 1/4 cups onion, diced
2 tablespoons margarine
1 cup cracker meal

Mix crabmeat, eggs, bread crumbs, spices, mayonnaise, and cheese until a good consistency is built. Add more bread crumbs if needed. Sauté onions in margarine until tender; add to mixture.

Form 4-ounce crab ball, and pat gently into cakes. Pour cracker meal over cakes, covering entirely. Shake extra meal off. Sauté until golden. Serve with cocktail sauce.

Serves 6

Crab and Artichoke Spread

1 pound imitation crabmeat, chopped
3 cups canned artichoke hearts, drained and chopped
2 - 2 1/2 cups mayonnaise
3 shakes Tabasco sauce
2 shakes Worcestershire sauce
1/2 cup grated Parmesan cheese
2 pinches garlic powder
1/4 cup chopped green onion
salt and pepper to taste

Combine all ingredients in large mixing bowl and mix thoroughly. Spread on crackers or use as a dip for chips.

To serve hot: heat in a baking dish at 275 degrees for about 10 minutes. Top with 1/2 cup grated cheddar cheese.

Serves 8 to 10

Shrimp Creole

1/2 pound butter
3/4 cup diced onion
3/4 cup green pepper, diced
1 cup sliced mushrooms
1/4 cup chopped celery
1/2 cup flour
1 cup chicken stock
1/2 cup tomato paste
3 cups stewed tomatoes
1 bay leaf
1 tablespoon fresh parsley, chopped
1/2 teaspoon salt
2 dashes pepper
1/2 teaspoon basil
1/2 teaspoon cayenne pepper
2 cups boiled shrimp, peeled and deveined

Sauté all vegetables in butter. Add flour, chicken stock, stewed tomatoes, and tomato paste. Stir well. Add all spices. Simmer for 1 hour. Add boiled shrimp.

Serve over rice.

Serves 5

Whaler's Famous Seafood Salad

1 pound shrimp, cooked, peeled, and deveined
2 pounds orange roughy, boiled in saltwater until flaky
1/2 pound crabmeat, picked
2 cups Hellmann's Mayonnaise
1/2 teaspoon garlic powder
1 teaspoon Worcestershire sauce
2 green onions, chopped
2 stalks celery, chopped
1/8 cup fresh parsley, chopped
1/8 cup dried chives
1 tablespoon Jane's Crazy Mixed-Up Salt

Mix all ingredients together. Serve on top of lettuce leaves or any mixed salad. Also great as a sandwich spread.

Serves 8

Whaler's Famous Seafood Salad is one of the most popular items on the menu. It is also delicious when served warm in an au gratin dish topped with shredded cheese.

Maria's Frozen Punch

8 ounces orange juice
8 ounces pineapple juice
4 ounces 7-Up
1 shot grenadine
1 shot cherry juice
2 cups ice

Mix all ingredients except ice in blender. Add ice and blend. Garnish with pineapple slices or oranges.

Serves 2

Willow Pond Southern Catfish was founded by Dennis and Patricia Winn, Roger and Phyllis Sigler, and Charles and Wilma Edmonds in November 1991. Specializing in the Southern style of preparing catfish and hushpuppies, Willow Pond soon enjoyed a reputation for delicious food and hearty portions at prices geared to a family's budget.

After 16 months of successful operation at its Eddyville location, Willow Pond Southern Catfish opened its second location in Aurora. Shortly thereafter, a third location opened in Calvert City.

Almost immediately upon being seated in a Willow Pond Southern Catfish restaurant, customers are dished a heaping pile of all-you-can-eat hush puppies; vinegar- or mayonnaise-based coleslaw; sliced, sweet onions; tangy bean relish; and a generous bowl of Southern-style white beans. Within minutes the cooked-to-order, piping hot entrees are served.

The majority of Willow Pond patrons order the fish dinners that are the specialty of the house, choosing pond-raised catfish fillets or Icelandic ocean cod, which can be prepared fried, baked, grilled, or blackened in the Cajun style. Additional menu items include jumbo frog legs, grilled and battered chicken and shrimp, hearty sandwiches such as the popular ground sirloin Willow Burger, and steaks.

Willow Pond Southern Catfish

"For the small fry," a special menu is offered, featuring fish nuggets, chicken strips, shrimp, or a hamburger and fries. Homemade desserts include Grandma's Cobbler, big enough for two, the famous Fudge Brownie, and chocolate sundaes.

Along with its great food, Willow Pond is known for its friendly and courteous staff. Employees are unfailingly cheerful and enthusiastic, making sure the iced tea glasses are always full, and refilling the hush puppy bowl or bringing more white beans as requested. The wide-open dining rooms allow friends to talk back and forth to each other, and the family atmosphere encourages the happy banter between tables.

All in all, it would be hard to find a more authentic

down home dining experience than the one that awaits diners at Willow Pond Southern Catfish restaurants.

Proprietors: Charles and Wilma Edmonds, Roger and Phyllis Sigler, Dennis and Patricia Winn.

Address: P.O. Box 1073, Eddyville, KY 42038 (corporate headquarters).

Telephone: Eddyville: (502) 388-4354; Aurora: (502) 474-2202; Calvert City: (502) 395-7802.

Hours: 11:00 a.m. to 9:00 p.m. Monday through Saturday; Sunday from 11:00 a.m. to 9:00 p.m.

Season: Winter hours vary by location. Please call ahead and check.

Seating: No reservations necessary.

Credit cards: MasterCard, Visa, and Discover.

Directions: Eddyville: Take exit 40 off Interstate 24, then go two miles east on U.S. Highway 62. Aurora: U.S. Highway 68 near Kenlake State Park. Calvert City: U.S. Highway 62 off exit 27 of Interstate 24.

Willow Pond Vinegar Slaw

1 head cabbage, grated
1 carrot, grated
1 small onion, chopped
1/2 green pepper, chopped
1 1/4 cups sugar
2/3 cup white vinegar
2/3 cup salad oil
1/2 teaspoon whole celery seed
1 teaspoon salt

Mix cabbage, carrot, onion, and pepper. Set aside. In a saucepan, mix sugar, vinegar, salad oil, celery seed, and salt and bring to a boil. Set aside to cool.

Mix dressing with grated cabbage mixture and refrigerate.

Makes 25 servings

This delicious sweet and sour slaw is a favorite of Willow Pond customers! It is especially good when served with fish, and keeps well when refrigerated.

Southern–Style White Beans

4 cups dried white beans
1/4 ham hock
2 tablespoons salt
pepper to taste
water

Rinse beans. Place in pot and cover with approximately 4 inches of water. Bring to a boil. Add ham hock and salt and pepper. Reduce heat and simmer approximately 2 1/2 to 3 hours. Keep water level above beans throughout the cooking process.

Serves 15 to 20

Sweet Potato Casserole

1 No. 2 can sweet potatoes or 4 to 6 medium sweet
potatoes, cooked
1/2 cup Eagle Brand milk
1 cup sugar
2 teaspoons vanilla
3 eggs
1 stick margarine, softened

Topping:
1 cup brown sugar
1/2 cup self-rising flour
1 cup chopped pecans
1 stick margarine

Mash potatoes and add the milk, sugar, vanilla, eggs, and softened margarine. Pour into baking dish.

To make topping, cut margarine into sugar and flour. Stir in nuts and spread on top of potato mixture.

Bake at 300 degrees for 60 minutes.

Serves 4 to 6

Lemon Lush

Crust:
1 stick margarine, melted
1 cup self-rising flour
5 tablespoons sugar
1/2 cup finely chopped pecans

Bottom filling:
9 ounces Cool Whip
8 ounces cream cheese, softened
1 cup powdered sugar

Top filling:
2 small packages instant lemon pudding

Top layer:
Cool Whip
chopped pecans

To make the crust, combine the melted margarine, flour, sugar, and nuts. Press into bottom of 9 x 13 inch pan. Bake 15 minutes at 325 degrees, then let cool.

To make bottom filling, combine cream cheese, Cool Whip, and powdered sugar, mixing until smooth. Spread over cooled crust.

To make top filling, mix instant pudding according to package directions. Spread on top of filling.

To make top layer, spread Cool Whip on top. Sprinkle with chopped pecans.

Serves 12 to 15

Taco Casserole

1 pound ground beef
1 package taco seasoning
1 can cream-style corn
1 can chili beans
1 medium bag tortilla chips
1/2 cup cheddar cheese, shredded

Brown ground beef and drain. Mix taco seasoning, corn, and beans with juice into the meat. Crumble chips (any amount you like) into bottom of 2 quart casserole dish. Pour meat mixture over chips. Bake at 325 degrees for 20 minutes. Sprinkle shredded cheese on top and place back into the oven until cheese melts.

Serves 4 to 6

This is an easy-to-prepare supper dish that children love! Serve it with sour cream, taco sauce, or shredded lettuce and tomato for a nice embellishment to a hearty meal.

Index

Dressings and Sauces

Entrées - Beef and Pork

Kentucky: Dining by the Lakes

Mail to:
McClanahan Publishing House, Inc.
P. O. Box 100
Kuttawa, KY 42055

For Orders call TOLL FREE
1-800-544-6959
Visa & MasterCard accepted

Please send me _____ copies of

Kentucky: Dining by the Lakes @ $ 12.95 each_____
Postage & handling   3.50   _____
Kentucky residents add 6% sales tax @   .78 each_____

Total enclosed   _____

Make check payable to McClanahan Publishing House

Ship to:
NAME

_____

ADDRESS

_____

CITY _____ STATE _____ ZIP _____

Please Copy